Reach Your Potential
AQUARIUS

GW00775908

Teresa Moorey

Orders: please contact Bookpoint Ltd, 39 Milton Park, Abingdon, Oxon OX14 4TD. Telephone: (44) 01235 400414, Fax: (44) 01235 400454. Lines are open from 9.00–6.00, Monday to Saturday, with a 24 hour message answering service. Email address: orders@bookpoint.co.uk

British Library Cataloguing in Publication Data
A CIP record for this title is available from the British Library

ISBN 0 340 69719 9

First published 1998
Impression number 11   10   9   8   7   6   5   4   3   2
Year   2004   2003   2002   2001   2000   1999   1998

Copyright © 1998 Teresa Moorey

Typeset by Transet Limited, Coventry, England.
Printed in Great Britain for Hodder & Stoughton Educational, a division of Hodder Headline plc, 338 Euston Road, London NW1 3BH by Cox & Wyman, Reading, Berks.

Contents

Introduction

A PERSPECTIVE ON ASTROLOGY

Interest in the mystery and significance of the heavens is perhaps as old as humanity. If we can cast our imaginations back, to a time when there were no street lamps, televisions or even books, if we can picture how it must have been to have nothing to do through the deep nights of winter other than to sit and weave stories by the fire at the cave mouth, then we can come close to sensing how important the great dome of stars must have seemed in ancient times.

We are prone to believe that we are wiser today, having progressed beyond old superstitions. We know that all stars are like our Sun – giant nuclear reactors. We know that the planets are lumps of rock reflecting sunlight, they are not gods or demons. But how wise are we in truth? Our growing accumulation of facts brings us no closer to discovering the real meaning behind life. It may well be that our cave-dwelling ancestors knew better than us the meaning of holism. The study of astrology may be part of a journey towards a more holistic perception, taking us, as it does, through the fertile, and often uncharted realms of our own personality.

Until the seventeenth century astrology (which searches for the meaning of heavenly patterns) and astronomy (which seeks to clarify facts about the skies) were one, and it was the search for meanings, not facts that inspired the earliest investigations. Lunar phases have been found carved on bone and stone figures from as early as 15,000BCE (Before Common Era). Astrology then evolved through the civilisations of Mesopotamia and Greece, and others. Through the 'dark ages' much astrological lore was preserved in Islamic countries, but in the fifteenth century astrology grew in popularity in the West. Queen Elizabeth I had her own personal astrologer, John Dee, and such fathers of modern astronomy as Kepler and Galileo served as court astrologers in Europe.

Astrology was taught at the University of Salamanca until 1776. What is rarely appreciated is that some of our greatest scientists, notably Newton and even Einstein, were led to their discoveries by intuition. Newton was a true mystic, and it was the search for meaning – the same motivation that inspired the Palaeolithic observer – that gave rise to some of our most brilliant advances. Indeed Newton is widely believed to have been an astrologer. The astronomer Halley, who discovered the famous comet, is reported to have criticised Newton for this, whereupon Sir Isaac replied 'I have studied it Sir, you have not!'

During the twentieth century astrology enjoyed a revival, and in 1948 The Faculty of Astrological Studies was founded, offering tuition of high quality and an examination system. The great psychologist Carl Jung was a supporter of astrology, and his work has expanded ideas about the mythic connections of the birth chart. Astrology is still eyed askance by many people, and there is no doubt that there is little purely scientific coroboration for astrology – the exception to this is the exhaustive statistical work undertaken by the Gauquelins. Michel Gauquelin was a French statistician whose research shows undeniable connection between professional prominence and the position of planets at birth. Now that the concept of a mechanical universe is being superseded, there is a greater chance that astrology and astronomy will reunite.

Anyone who consults a good astrologer comes away deeply impressed by the insight of the birth chart. Often it is possible to see very deeply into the personality and to be able to throw light on current dilemmas.

It is noteworthy that even the most sceptical of people tend to know their Sun sign and the characteristics associated with it.

■ WHAT IS A BIRTH CHART?

Your birth chart is a map of the heavens drawn up for the time, date and place of your birth. An astrologer will prefer you to be as accurate as you can about the time of day, for that affects the sign

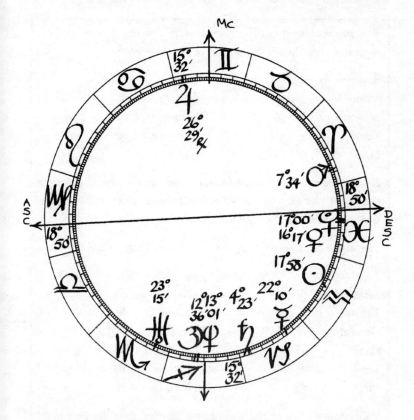

The birth chart of Charles Dickens
Dickens' Aquarian Sun gave him social awareness and a clear perspective on human life.

rising on the eastern horizon. This 'rising sign' is very important to your personality. However, if you do not know your birth time a chart can still be compiled for you. There will be some details missing, but useful interpretations may still be made. It is far better for the astrologer to know that your birth time is in question than to operate from a position of false certainty. The birth chart for Charles Dickens (page 3) is a simplified chart. Additional factors would be entered on the chart and considered by an astrologer, such as angles (aspects) between the planets, and the houses.

The **planets** are life principles, energy centres. To enable you to understand the birth chart, here are their glyphs:

Sun	⊙	Jupiter	♃
Moon	☽	Saturn	♄
Mercury	☿	Uranus	♅
Venus	♀	Neptune	♆
Mars	♂	Pluto	♇ (℗)

Rising Sign or **Ascendant** (**ASC**) is the way we have of meeting the world, our outward persona. **Midheaven** (**MC**) refers to our image, aspirations, how we like to be seen.

The **signs** are modes of expression, ways of being. Here are their glyphs:

Aries	♈	Libra	♎
Taurus	♉	Scorpio	♏
Gemini	♊	Sagittarius	♐
Cancer	♋	Capricorn	♑
Leo	♌	Aquarius	♒
Virgo	♍	Pisces	♓

Using knowledge of the glyphs you can see that the Sun is in Gemini in our example birth chart (page 3).

The birth chart shows each of the planets and the Moon in the astro-logical signs, and can be thought of as an 'energy map' of the different forces operating within the psyche. Thus the Sun sign (often called 'birth sign' or 'star sign') refers only to the position of the Sun. If the planets are in very different signs from the Sun sign, the interpretation will be greatly modified. Thus, if a person has Sun in Leo yet is somewhat introverted or quiet, this may be because the Moon was in reserved Capricorn when that person was born. Nonetheless, the Sun represents the light of consciousness, the inte-grating force, and most people recognise that they are typical of their Sun sign, although in some people it will be more noticeable than in others. The planets Mercury and Venus are very close to the Sun and often occupy the same sign, so intensifying the Sun-sign influence.

This book is written about your Sun sign, because the Sun sign serves as an accessible starting point for those wishing to learn about themselves through astrology. However, do not let your interest stop there. If you find anything helpful in comments and advice stemming from Sun sign alone, you will find your true birth chart even more revealing. The address of the Faculty of Astrological Studies appears in 'Further Reading' at the back of this book, and it is a good idea to approach them for a list of trained astrologers who can help you. Moon *phase* at birth (as distinct from Moon sign) is also very important. *The Moon and You for Beginners* (see 'Further Reading') explains this fascinating area clearly, and provides a sim-ple chart for you to look up your Moon phase, and learn what this means for your personality.

■ HOW DOES ASTROLOGY WORK?

We cannot explain astrology by the usual methods of cause and effect. In fact, there are many things we cannot explain. No one can define exactly what life is. We do not know exactly what electricity is, but we know how to use it. Few of us have any idea how a television set works, but we know how to turn it on. Although we are not able to explain astrology we are still able to use it, as any capable astrologer will demonstrate.

Jung discovered something called 'synchronicity'. This he defined as 'an acausal connecting principle'. Simply, this means that some events have a meaningful connection *other than cause and effect*. The planets do not cause us to do things, but their movements are synchronistic with our lives. The old dictum 'as above, so below' applies here. It is a mystery. We can't explain it, but that doesn't mean we should refuse to believe in it. A little boy on a visit to the circus saw an elephant for the first time and said 'There's no such thing'. We may laugh at the little boy, but how many of us respond to things we do not understand in this way?

The planetary positions in your birth chart are synchronistic with the time of your birth, when you took on separate existence, and they are synchronistic with your individuality in this life. They have much to say about you.

■ MYTH AND PSYCHOLOGY

The planets are named after the old gods and goddesses of Rome, which in turn link in with Greek and other pantheons. The planets represent 'life principles' – forces that drive the personality, and as such they can be termed 'archetypal'. This means that they are basic ideas, universal within human society and are also relevant in terms of the forces that, in some inexplicable way, inhabit the corners of the universe and inform the Earth and all human institutions. Thus the assertive energy that is represented by Mars means energetic action of all sorts – explosions and fires, wars, fierce debates and personal anger. Put briefly, here are the meanings of the planets:

- Mercury – intellect and communication
- Venus – love, unifying, relating
- Mars – assertion, energy, fighting spirit
- Jupiter – expansion, confidence, optimism
- Saturn – limitation, discipline
- Uranus – rebellion, independence
- Neptune – power to seek the ideal, sense the unseen
- Pluto – power to transform and evolve

These principles are modified according to the astrological sign they inhabit, thus Venus in Pisces may be gently loving, dreamy and self-sacrificing while Venus in Aries will be demanding and adventurous in relationships. Thus the planets in signs form a complex psychological framework – and that is only part of the story of chart interpretation!

In the old mythologies these 'energies' or 'archetypes' or 'gods' were involved in classical dramas. An example is the story of Saturn and Uranus. This is particularly relevant to Aquarius as we shall see. Uranus is the rejecting father of Saturn, who later castrates and murders his father – thus innovative people reject reactionaries, who then murder them, so the revolutionary part of the personality is continually 'killed off' by the restrictive part. The exact positions and angles between the planets will indicate how this and other myths may come to life. In addition, the mere placement of planets by sign – and, of course, especially the Sun sign, call forth various myths as illustrations. The ancient myths are good yarns but they are inspired and vivid dramatisations of what may be going on repeatedly within your personality and that of your nearest and dearest. Myths are used by many modern psychologists and therapists in a tradition that has grown since Jung. We shall be using mythic themes to illustrate internal dynamics in this book.

SIGN	QUALITY	ELEMENT
Aries	Cardinal	Fire
Taurus	Fixed	Earth
Gemini	Mutable	Air
Cancer	Cardinal	Water
Leo	Fixed	Fire
Virgo	Mutable	Earth
Libra	Cardinal	Air
Scorpio	Fixed	Water
Sagittarius	Mutable	Fire
Capricorn	Cardinal	Earth
Aquarius	Fixed	Air
Pisces	Mutable	Water

■ THE SIGNS OF THE ZODIAC

There are twelve signs, and each of these belongs to an Element –
Earth, Fire, Air or Water, and a Quality – Cardinal, Fixed or
Mutable. The Cardinal signs are more geared to action, the Fixed
tend to remain stable and rooted, whereas the Mutable signs are
adaptable, changeable.

Jung defined four functions of consciousness – four different ways of
perceiving the world – 'thinking', 'feeling', 'sensation' and
'intuition'. Thinking is the logical, evaluative approach that works in
terms of the mind. Feeling is also evaluative, but this time in relation
to culture and family needs. This is not the same as emotion, although
'feeling' people often process emotions more smoothly than other
types. Jung saw 'feeling' as rational, too. 'Sensation' refers to the 'here
and now', the five physical senses, while 'intuition' relates to lives in
terms of the possible, to visions and hunches. Jung taught that we
tend to have one function uppermost in consciousness, another one

or maybe two secondary and another repressed or 'inferior', although we all possess each of these functions to some degree.

Jungian ideas are being refined and expanded, and they are incorporated into modern methods of personality testing, as in the Myers-Briggs test. If a prospective employer has recently given you such a test, it was to establish your talents and potential for the job. However, the basic four-fold division is still extremely useful, and I find that it is often of great help in assisting clients to understand themselves, and their partners, in greater depth – for we are all apt to assume that everyone processes information and applies it in the same way as we do. But they don't! It is worthy of mention that the important categories of 'introverted' and 'extraverted' were also identified by Jung. In astrology, Fire and Air signs seem to be extraverted, generally speaking, and Earth and Water introverted – and this has been borne out by the statistical research of the astrologer, Jeff Mayo. However, this doesn't mean that all feeling and sensation people are introverted and all intuitives and thinkers extraverted – this is definitely not the case, and calls for more detailed examination of the chart (e.g. lots of Fire and Water may mean an extravert feeling type).

Very broadly speaking we may link the Fire signs to intuition, Water to feeling, Earth to sensation and Air to thinking. Often thinking and feeling are drawn together and sensation and intuition are attracted, because they are opposites. This probably happens because we all seek to become more whole, but the process can be painful. The notion of the four functions, when understood, does help to throw light on some of the stumbling blocks we often encounter in relationships. However, some people just do not seem to fit. Also Fire doesn't always correspond to intuition, Water to feeling, etc. – it seems this is usually the case, but not all astrologers agree. Some link Fire with feeling, Water with intuition, and most agree that other chart factors are also important. As with all theories, this can be used to help, expand and clarify, not as a rigid system to impose definitions. We shall be learning more about these matters in relation to the Sun sign in the following pages.

■ THE PRECESSION OF THE EQUINOXES

One criticism often levelled at astrology is that 'the stars have moved' and so the old signs are invalid. There is some truth in this, and it is due to a phenomenon called 'The Precession of the Equinoxes'. The beginning of the sign Aries occurs when the Sun is overhead at the equator, moving northwards. This is called the Spring Equinox, for now day and night are equal all over the globe, and the first point of Aries is called the 'equinoctial point'. Because the Earth not only turns on its axis but 'rocks' on it (imagine a giant knitting needle driven through the poles – the Earth spins on this, but the head of the needle also slowly describes a circle in space) the 'equinoctial point' has moved against the background of stars. Thus, when the Sun is overhead at the equator, entering Aries, it is no longer at the start of the constellation of Aries, where it occurred when the signs were named, but is now in the constellation of Pisces. The 'equinoctial point' is moving backwards into Aquarius, hence the idea of the dawning 'Aquarian age'.

So where does that leave astrology? Exactly in the same place, in actuality. For it all depends on how you think the constellations came to be named in the first place. Did our ancestors simply look up and see the shape of a Ram in the sky? Or did they – being much more intuitive and in tune with their surroundings than we are – feel sharply aware of the quality, the energies around at a certain time of the year, and *then* look skywards translating what they sensed into a suitable starry symbol? This seems much more likely – and you have only to look at the star groups to see that it takes a fair bit of imagination to equate most of them with the figures they represent! The Precession of the Equinoxes does not affect astrological interpretation, for it is based upon observation and intuition, rather than 'animals in the sky'.

■ USING THIS BOOK

Reach Your Potential – Aquarius explores your Sun sign and what this means in terms of your personality; the emphasis is on self-exploration. All the way through, hints are given to help you to begin to understand yourself better, ask questions about yourself and use what you have to maximum effect. This book will show you how to use positive Aquarian traits to your best advantage, and how to neutralise negative Aquarian traits. Don't forget that by reading it you are consenting, however obliquely, to the notion that you are connected in strange and mysterious ways to the web of the cosmos. What happens within you is part of a meaningful pattern that you can explore and become conscious of, thereby acquiring greater influence on the course of your life. Let this encourage you to ask further questions.

Some famous Aquarians

Martin Shaw, Beatrice Webb (British socialist), Angela Davis (revolutionary), Germaine Greer, Elizabeth Blackwell (first woman doctor to qualify), Virginia Wolfe, Colette, Gertrude Stein, Lucy Irvine, Kathy Ford, Francis Bacon, Tallulah Bankhead, John Barrymore, Jack Benny, George Burns, Lewis Caroll, Katherine Cornell, Charles Darwin, James Dean, Charles Dickens, Jimmy Durante, Thomas Edison, Mia Farrow, Clark Gable, Galileo, Jack Lemmon, Abraham Lincoln, Charles Lindbergh, Somerset Maugham, Jeanne Moreau, Paul Newman, Kim Novak, Ronald Reagan, Vanessa Redgrave, Franklin D. Roosevelt, James Joyce, Frederick Delius, Anna Pavlova, Christian Dior.

Water Bearer, Water Sprinkler or Grecian Urn – what sort of Aquarius are you?

Here is a quiz to give you an idea of how you are operating at the moment. Its tone is light hearted, but the intent is serious and you may find out something interesting about yourself. Don't think too hard about the answers, just pick the one that appeals to you most.

1. **The emotional life of a close friend is in disarray and he or she is deeply upset. How do you think you might react?**

   a) ☐ Give lots of resourceful advice, and go round at odd times to see how your friend is and to give more advice. (It's funny, the car was on the drive last time you called and you could have sworn you saw a curtain move, but no one came to the door . . .)

   b) ☐ Tell your friend exactly what to do: 'It's quite obvious s/he's no good for you/that dog isn't going to recover. Get rid of her/him/have it put down, and get on with life.' When your advice isn't followed your patience wears thin.

   c) ☐ You know you aren't at your best when it comes to being sympathetic and it grieves you to see your friend like this. You tell your friend where to find you if you are needed, and you make arrangements to meet up for a drink. Meanwhile you feel it's best to give your friend space.

2. **Your new boss bawls you out in front of everyone for something minor. How might you react?**

   a) ☐ You probably wouldn't react. You'd tell yourself you don't care.

   b) ☐ You might say and do nothing at the time, but you would instantly begin looking for another post. You don't need that sort of thing.

c) ❏ You've never worked for that sort of boss, but if it happened, you'd walk out on the spot.

3. **You have a secret assignation to keep, throbbing with excitement. Just as you are about to leave a friend turns up in a state of near hysteria, needing your help. Now what do you do?**

a) ❏ You split your time. Your friend goes off muttering about jumping in the canal and your lover is angry and uncomprehending. What is the matter with everyone?

b) ❏ You go to see your lover, but insist on phoning your friend several times and talking incessantly about the problem.

c) ❏ The needs of the moment call. You get a message to your lover if you can and devote the rest of the evening to trying to cheer up your friend.

4. **You have a long-term relationship with a fairly needy partner, but you have to admit there are things lacking – in fact, some might call the relationship 'dead'. What are you going to do about it?**

a) ❏ If there's a relationship, if you're still talking, then how can it be dead? (The thought of admitting such a thing makes you shudder.)

b) ❏ You'd stay, in all probability. Duty and friendship are the most important things and you have no strong needs of your own.

c) ❏ You can't imagine ever being in such a situation.

5. **You have a great new plan to build your own radio telescope/recycle cellophane packets/house the local homeless. However, when you try to tell your circle of friends they hardly listen, and even make fun of you. What do you do?**

a) ❏ You shut up and keep your ideas to yourself. Inwardly you despise them, and feel isolated.

b) ❏ You argue doggedly and earnestly, ignoring the banter.

c) ☐ If you have an important project you usually execute it alone. You wouldn't bother with people who weren't prepared to listen and think.

6. **Apparently you have a snobby neighbour who drives a flash car and ignores you – actually you wouldn't have noticed had this not been pointed out to you by another neighbour, but now you know, how do you react?**

a) ☐ It doesn't matter – you love everyone anyway.

b) ☐ You spend some time analysing the neighbours behaviour and decide he or she must have a severe problem with an underlying inferiority complex.

c) ☐ Why on earth would it matter? You honestly couldn't care less.

7. **At work, your sphere of influence is extended and you are given the task of opening a new department or branch. What does this mean to you?**

a) ☐ It's okay, but not that important. You wouldn't let it preoccupy you.

b) ☐ You'd relish the chance for more independence and autonomy, and the chance to put some of your ideas into practice.

c) ☐ It's most unlikely you'd do the sort of work where that would happen. You have – and need – considerable autonomy anyway.

8. **You are watching a film/performance/television programme with your friends and, despite having agreed to be present, you find it boring. Meanwhile everyone else is absorbed. What do you do?**

a) ☐ You watch and disrupt by turns.

b) ☐ You endure politely.

c) ☐ You quietly leave.

9. **Despite your flair and inspired input you have been passed over for a promotion that should have been yours. How do you react?**

   a) ☐ You tell yourself the job is rubbish and act erratically – you can't be bothered to co-operate any more.

   b) ☐ You tell yourself you must rise above this setback and carry on regardless.

   c) ☐ It would be very unlikely that such a thing would matter that much – you have other plans.

Now count up your score. What do you have most of – a's, b's or c's?

Mostly a's. At the moment you are rather the 'Grecian Urn' type of Aquarius: lovely profile but hollow. It is hard for you to face up to how you feel or to being powerless in certain situations, but you have not quite given yourself permission to be a free spirit. You may tell yourself you are detached, but is that really true? Because of this many ordinary situations faze you somewhat, and you are capable of acting a little cranky and haywire – it is hard for you to 'water' the spiritual soil of yourself or anyone else. However, you have all the Aquarian originality and detachment – when are you going to make it work for you?

Mostly b's. You seem to be the 'Water Sprinkler' type at present. You can be rather witholding emotionally and very bound by doing the 'right thing'. You probably have strong ideals and principles, but how emotionally 'free' are you able to be – or to let your associates be? You are to some extent the more 'Saturnian' Aquarius that we shall be describing in the following pages. Although you may be fairly effectual it is unlikely that you feel fulfilled. You 'sprinkle' your Aquarian gems, but they fall somewhat thin. Perhaps you should think of trading that straight-jacket for something more fitted to the twenty-first century.

Mostly c's. You are the 'Water Bearer' type of Aquarius. You are your 'own person' – highly original, independent and self-motivating. You quite honestly do not care about, or notice many of the things that bother other people. However, you are a source of inspiration to yourself and others, and you liberally provide the conceptual 'Waters' that are the gift of your sign. The only drawback may be that you find it hard to understand what makes some of the human race tick, and you may feel isolated at times. Try to get to know yourself emotionally as well as theoretically – it will make all your attempts relevant as well as revolutionary.

If you found that in many cases none of the answers came any-where near to fitting you, then it may be that you are an uncharacteristic Aquarius. This may be because there are factors in your astrological chart that frustrate the expression of your Sun sign, or it may be because there is a preponderance of other signs, outweighing the Aquarius part. Whatever the case may be, your Sun-sign potential needs to be realised. Perhaps you will find something to help ring a few bells in the following pages.

1 The essential Aquarius

Yet, Freedom! yet thy banner, torn, but flying,
Streams like the thunder-storm against the wind

Byron, *Childe Harold's Pilgrimage*

I intend no modification of my oft expressed
personal wish that all men everywhere could be free.

Abraham Lincoln

■ HERALDS OF THE NEW AGE

Most of us are familiar with the lines from the rock musical, *Hair* that tell us

> *When the Moon is in the seventh house*
> *and Jupiter aligns with Mars,*
> *then peace will guide the planets,*
> *and love will steer the stars.*
> *This is the dawning of the age of Aquarius . . .*

The 1960s 'flower power' that spawned these lyrics is history, but there persists, nonetheless, a belief that we are poised on the threshold of the 'Age of Aquarius' – a fresh and challenging time, when the tired and fusty will be blown away on the winds of change. The light of true freedom will show the route to progress for a human race destined to evolve into a higher state of awareness. There is a thirst for a new experience, the insistence on thinking for ourselves and departing from the catechisms of our forbears, and the uncovering of new meanings in ancient wisdom teachings – all Aquarian themes. The demolition of the Berlin Wall, the parting of the Iron Curtain and the death of apartheid are some of the events that have proclaimed the new vision. Crystals, 'earth mysteries', astrology, dream interpretation, meditation, shamanism and spiritual healing are just a few of the areas of personal exploration. A time of excitement and brilliant new horizons, or a confusing phase of rainbow chasing, self-delusion and even destruction?

There are many ways of looking at the 'New Age' – and indeed for many parts of the globe there are no new freedoms or ideas, but just an ancient bondage to fear and famine that has increased, rather than receded, with modern weapons of warfare. 'Developed' nations also have some unspiritual problems in the shape of homelessness and joblessness. Opinions vary on what so-called enlightenment can mean for the Western world – some are sceptical while others are enthusiastic. And what might all of this have to do with those who are 'Aquarians'? One thing is for certain: such issues are the concern of the average Aquarius, and they are reflected upon and debated with great interest by all who have Aquarius strong in the natal chart.

The 'Age of Aquarius' expresses the current 'zeitgeist' and our millenarian dreams, but it is also an astronomical phenomenon related to the movement of the equinoctial point (see page 10) backwards into the constellation of Aquarius, and while the apparent characteristics of the dawning age seem to have much in common with Aquarian ideals, this New Age – if New Age there is – is a factor in the lives of all of us, not merely Aquarians. Having said this, the dilemmas of the current situation are apparent in Aquarius as a sign. Some Aquarians are true iconoclasts and would be happy to blast all tradition into eternity at the touch of a button. Others are more reactionary – this results, in part, from the 'dual' rulership of Aquarius by Saturn and Uranus, which we shall be examining later.

However, even the concept of 'freedom' itself – so dear to the Aquarian heart – contains its own paradoxes and contradictions, and these are central to the Aquarian personality: for instance, are we 'free' to disagree on the subject of universal brotherhood? Who sweeps the streets while we pursue 'crystals and light'? And what about our all-too-human feelings of envy, competition, desire . . . ? Are they 'free' to see the light of day? Or should they be buried in a crypt of guilt, under an ivory tower?

It is fitting to begin our consideration of Aquarius in the context of wider social and humanitarian matters, because such is so often the orientation of Aquarius. Freedom loving, idealistic, original and humanitarian, this is the sign of the Reformer, of the person who loves the sisterhood and brotherhood of humanity, yet often shrinks from rubbing shoulders with grubby mortals. Louis XIVth of France articulated the Aquarian dilemma when he stated that he did not mind being baptised by the waters of universal suffrage but he did not want to live with his feet in them! Aquarius wants equality for all – as long as personal freedom is not thereby restricted. There are many ambiguities to this complex and sometimes contradictory sign of the Utopian.

■ AQUARIUS BODY LANGUAGE

There is usually something slightly whacky or unconventional about Aquarian appearance. 'Ethnic' clothes are often favoured, and some Aquarians are proud of the fact that they dress themselves from jumble sales, which may be readily apparent! Aquarians can look as if their clothes leapt, unironed from the laundry basket and swathed themselves about their abstracted selves – except that even the laws of chance could surely not bring about such an ill-assorted rag doll! Some Aquarians manage to dress the top half as if it didn't belong to the bottom half – co-ordination may stop at the waist. Some are plain scruffy, while the disregard of others for the impression they create amounts to a two fingers to the world gesture (and secretly shows that they care very much to be seen as not caring!). For the average Aquarius, appearance is more subtle, and there may be merely something unusual or intriguing about your demeanour. Aquarian women, in particular, are often capable of creating their own, unmistakeable style, that may be the envy of others who shop in chain stores and look on in mystification at the Water Bearer's *je ne sais quoi.*

The 'mad professor' archetype, portrayed in films such as *Young Einstein* or as the Doctor in *Back to the Future* is the most Aquarian. You Aquarians may not look precisely as if you have your finger stuck in an electric socket, but there may be something highly strung and definitely zany about you. Movements may be abrupt, speech brusque and appearance angular. There may be a far-away expression, and a restlessness that may manifest as fidgeting or may be more a case of swift response to any call to explore, mentally or physically. Aquarians may go from nought to sixty in a matter of seconds, especially if bored. However, in the vast majority of Aquarians these traits are noticeable only on close examination. Some are capable of a statuesque stillness. Suffice to say that there is often an 'off planet' impression, given by manner or action, that indicates the Aquarian is not fully earth-bound. Some are almost unbelievably absent-minded (but the more 'Saturnian' are circumspect). There may be an all-or-nothing quality to their attention, but even while one is under the spotlight, one knows that it may move on at any time. You Aquarians are interesting and unpredictable people, but as in all cases, Rising Sign is important in influencing mannerisms, and Aquarian characteristics are likely to be greatly modified by other chart factors.

■ MYTHS OF THE WATER BEARER

Aquarius is depicted as a human figure – generally male – emptying water from a jar. The water is a gift to the parched earth, or to a thirsty human or beast. One thing that is not portrayed is the Water Bearer receiving any of the water himself. It is important to remember that, despite the flowing symbol, Aquarius is an Air sign. The waters brought by Aquarius are those of enlightenment. The outpouring is of universal, not personal, love, and ironically it is often the Aquarian him or herself who 'runs on empty'. The detachment of Aquarius may keep human warmth to some extent at arm's length, and you may sacrifice yourselves – not in order to be absorbed in the mystical, or for any person or thing, but for your ideals.

Hapi, Hebe and Ganymede

Myths relating to the Water Bearer are not plentiful or clear. Our estrangement from the instinctual and the realms of the mother Goddess are reflected in the 'thinness' of the image. Water, after all, is the source of all life and we all begin existence in the cradle of amnoitic fluid that is the womb. In a sense, Aquarius is concerned with the waters of birth, as new consciousness dawns upon the infant in the cascade of birth fluid. In Egypt Aquarius was Hapi, the god of the flowing waters of the Nile, which flooded when the moon was full in Aquarius (and, thus, the Sun was in Leo). Some writers have linked Aquarius with the Olympian cup-bearers. Hebe was the first of these, pouring the gift of eternal life in the nectar from the jug, until one day she fell over and exposed her genitals. In ancient times times this would have been seen as a sacred act, for the sick were healed by the sight of the exposed sexual organs of the Goddess. However, the patriarchal Olympians were embarrassed by this, and Hebe's position was taken over by Ganymede, the boy-lover of Zeus.

This is one of many tales of the usurpation of the power of the feminine by masculinity. It may be the key to some of the Aquarian difficulties, for only by appreciating the essence of feminine, feeling virtues can Aquarius truly bring the gift of a love and wisdom that is particular, as well as collective, and that has practical application as well as theoretical validity. Profound 'knowingness' is a gift of Sophia, the Divine Mind, and it comes from the heart, the soul and even the gut – not merely from the thinking apparatus. In our scientific culture it has been all too easy for Aquarius to amputate these origins in favour of 'head stuff'. However, the truly wise Aquarian strives also to be conscious of his or her feelings, so there may be conviction and love behind reformative projects.

■ ELEMENT, QUALITY AND RULING PLANET

We have seen that each of the signs of the zodiac belongs to one of the Elements, Earth, Fire, Air or Water, and one of the Qualities, Cardinal, Fixed or Mutable. Aquarius is Fixed Air. This means that thinking, reflecting and analysing are important to the Aquarian temperament, and while you have a reputation for unpredictability, you can be stubborn to the point of dogmatism in matters of principle. The rather contradictory combination of 'Fixity' with the indefinability of Air renders the Aquarian character quite ambiguous, for while you are changeable, open to new concepts and even revolutionary in some cases, there is an inaccessibility about you. You love to communicate, even proselytise, but you may not listen. You are generally mobile and yet often inflexible.

We have seen that the Element of Air has some things in common with what Jung called the 'thinking' function. Thinking is about the use of the logical, analytical part of the human make-up, evaluating everything on the basis of detached thought. This approach has brought us untold benefits in the shape of scientific progress and has been responsible for the reflective approach to the human condition as a whole that has wrought so many social reforms. However, what is neglected in this orientation is a whole set of values that are equally 'rational' in their way, yet emphasise emotions, family bonds and personal perspectives – and these represent and vitalise the very 'humanity' prized by thinkers, in the abstract. Rampant 'thinking' without recourse to other value systems, has brought us all the current perils of global destruction that progress without real caring has caused. This is so often evident in the Aquarian perspective, where the essence of an idea may be put before the people it is intended to benefit. Aquarians may need to remind themselves that how people feel, however irrational this may be, *matters*, and that no one can or should be told how to feel on the basis of an ideal. Principles are meaningless without basic humanity, just as individuals may be rudderless without principles. Our culture is unbalanced in favour of 'thinking' and it is an enlightened Aquarius indeed, who sees the merit of redressing this.

Aquarius is the eleventh sign of the zodiac. The astrological year commences with the Pioneering spirit of Fiery Aries, followed by Taurus, the Settler and Farmer and Gemini, the Communicator. Then comes Cancer, sign of the Tribe and Family, and all the values so entailed, and then Leo, the Monarch. Virgo comes next, the Reaper and Sorter, followed by Libra, the Diplomat and sign of Relationships. Scorpio, sign of Passion and Transformation, is followed by Sagittarius, the Philosopher and then Capricorn, the Builder. This brings us up to date with Aquarius, the Reformer. Human society takes shape in a journey through the zodiac, and a point of review is arrived at, in a sense. The request is almost complete. What has been achieved? And what must be changed, viewed from a new perspective, eradicated and rebuilt? These are Aquarian questions.

Aquarius, in the Northern Hemisphere, marks a time of rebirth. This has been called the Cleansing Tide, when winter is in its final throes and the gradually increasing light, the whiteness of frost and the bleached skies of February tell us a New Age is on the way. The ancient feast of Imbolc is celebrated at the beginning of February (also called Candlemas). Now life stirs in the belly of the earth and creativity of all sorts is emphasised. The Goddess Bride is now revered – patroness of childbirth, poetry and smithcraft – and traditionally this was the festival when priestesses were initiated. Initiation, awakening, creating – these are Aquarian matters. However, for those of you living in the Southern Hemisphere, this is harvest time, when the first harbingers of the coming winter can be detected in the air. Aquarius thus heralds the increasing detachment of life and a time for growing reflection, as winter approaches. The waters of the Water Bearer thus bless the harvest. Now the old year begins to die – what is not needed or has passed its 'sell-by date' must be superseded, eventually to make way for a new vision, brought by Aquarius.

Each sign is said to have a 'Ruling Planet'. This means that there is a planet that has a special affinity with the sign, whose energies are most at home when expressed in terms of that sign. The Ruling Planet for Aquarius is Uranus, the Sky God, the Awakener. It seems that the astronomical discovery of a planet coincides with the emergence into the consciousness of humankind, of the energies connected with that planet. The discovery of Uranus in 1781 marked the upheavals of the French Revolution, the independence of America and the struggle against slavery. Following this came the dawn of a 'new age' in technology – electricity, radio and magnetic fields – and it is interesting to note that in Britain the first aerials were fashioned in the shape of the Uranus symbol ♅! Uranus may be seen as the planet of the magician, and there is something magical about the unseen rays that are translated to sounds and pictures in our domestic devices. Later the element Uranium was used for nuclear fission, releasing another kind of power, which was used in a most destructive way. However, prior to the discovery of the planet Uranus, Saturn was considered to be the ruler of Aquarius. Saturn is 'Old Father Time', the disciplinarian of the zodiac, marker of boundaries and setter of limits, culling, crystallising, giving shape and form but denoting burdens and hardship, as well as achievement. In some ways Saturn and Uranus are opposites – and we shall be recounting their mythic struggle in the following pages. Some Aquarians are more strongly Saturnian, while others are Uranian, but in every Aquarius both elements have a place. It will be seen that repressive Saturn was a rebel in his time and that idealistic Uranus was also a despot. Perhaps the two are not so very different underneath! Certainly, it is the aim of every Aquarius to identify with the positive traits of each.

■ SACRED COWS ON STAMPEDE

Aquarius is no lover of tradition for its own sake. 'We do it that way because that's how it's always been done' is the sort of remark calculated to send the average Aquarius into paroxysms of scorn or an orgy of idol smashing. Aquarius slaughters sacred cows. This can be very uncomfortable for anyone caught in the Uranian orbit – and if the truth were known, it's none too pleasant for Aquarius, who may fall foul of all and sundry in her or his attempts to better the condition of everyone concerned. Aquarians may tell themselves they don't care, but actually Aquarius does care what people think. Possibly the best way to express this is that Aquarians care quite desperately what people think *if they share their ideals.* Thus, it may be possible to shrug one's shoulders derisively at some accusations – being called 'over-idealistic' just shows the short-sightedness of the accuser, being called a 'rebel' is a compliment and four-letter words merely demonstrate that someone can't control his or her temper –

other epithets may be less desirable. Aquarius hates to be thought unfeeling, bigoted or attention seeking. Some would almost rather die than admit to jealousy, meanness and resentment. Because of this Aquarius, the noble and upstanding, can be surprisingly weak on occasion and will compromise ideals in order to create the right impression.

Such considerations, however, do not cloud the sight of an Aquarius on the trail of reform. You Aquarians are often years ahead of your time. You see things for what they are, without the trappings. You do not care for comfort, preferences, inertia or Auld Lang Syne. You see new vistas illuminated in a lightning flash. You are prophetic and intuitive.

It is no blessing being the only sighted person in the country of the blind and it is a sad thing that many Aquarian visions are left to starve in a dungeon of prejudice. Frustrating, too, for Aquarius, who may earnestly wonder why it is that no one else can *see* it, when it seems so clear. However, sometimes this is a case of 'everyone's out of step except my Johnny'. Aquarius does not appreciate the importance of human feelings as part of the equation. We are complex creatures, and while perhaps we should see certain things, face them, make changes, sometimes there are sound reasons why we don't. Yes, these may be because of prejudice, ignorance or fear of change. But some-times other values abound, such as aesthetics, group bonding, familiarity and respect. Fact and logic are no substitute for meaning – something which intuitive Aquarius can be brought to appreciate.

By no means all Aquarians are so extreme, and there are plenty who embrace a relatively conventional lifestyle with never a whiff or rebel-lion. However, it is a rare Aquarian who does not seek to make changes of one sort or another, and some may be suspected of adopt-ing change for change's sake. Aquarians may be puzzled and hurt by the rejection of their ideas, designed to benefit all and sundry.

■ EXPECTING THE UNEXPECTED

Aquarius is an unpredictable sign. Often you are unwilling to commit yourself to an engagement because you realise that you do not know how you may feel tomorrow, or what notion may grip you. The effect of Aquarius on companions can be galvanic and inspiring, or it can be chaotic. Some Aquarians seem incapable of leaving the house wearing matching socks – and some do quite well to remember their shoes! Strongly Aquarian or Uranian individuals often have more than a hint of genius – and we all know the saying that the line between genius and madness is a fine one indeed! However, it may not be just Aquarius who is 'mad'. Spouses, employers and hostesses may be driven to the brink by an Aquarius who pops up at all sorts of odd times.

Some 'unpredictability' stems from a preoccupation with other, deeper matters, and some arises from the inspirational Aquarian mind-set, where a sudden 'flash' may set Aquarius off on some adventure. In the vast majority of Aquarians nothing so dramatic is visible, and there may simply be the tendency to express the occasional unusual viewpoint, or sometimes to turn up late. Some members of the sign have to 'do the right thing' almost obsessively. Mixed with what is generally an independent and even unusual personality, this can be hard to understand. However, the more 'Saturnian' Aquarian is deeply concerned with duty.

Aquarius as a sign has a dislike of being petty or driven (even the teeniest bit) by emotion. Some are quite terrified of feelings, although this tends to apply much less to Aquarian women, who are more into controlling them. This sign likes – needs – to be 'above it all'. Because of this, doing one's 'duty' however one may define it, can be a soft option. It is easier to decide upon a code of principles and to stick to them, come hell or high passion, than to be cast out upon the stormy seas of feelings. Preoccupied by ideas and ethics, not wanting your visions to be tarnished by your own humanity, you can play the noble soul to the detriment of your own peace of mind. A simple example of this is the person who stays in a dead marriage, making mincemeat of his or her own emotions, rather than face a divorce and the accusation, even if only a self-accusation, of selfishness.

So it can be a mistake to describe all Aquarians as unpredictable. If the truth were known, some are far too predictable for their own good. There is a lot to be said for the 'unpredictability' of Aquarius. Those of an esoteric bent might call this 'a sudden response to input from the Universal Mind' while others speak of independence and individualism. On thing is for sure – Aquarius can be exciting, and galvanically so. This is the spirit that said 'Why should the world be flat, just because everyone says so' and discovered America. This is the sign of the Great Awakener, tailor-made to shake us out of our sleep and into a reality beyond our dreams. Aquarius, great at speaking up for liberty, needs sometimes to find a real liberty for themselves. Unpredictability can be a small price to pay for those treated to the first glimpse of new continents.

▮ NOT SO HIGH AND NOBLE

Our next section may not be an easy one to read, or even to understand, for many Aquarians. This is because we are going to talk about the 'seamy side' of the sign, and Aquarius is dedicated to avoiding anything seamy, especially in themselves. There is no doubt that Aquarius is noble, high-minded and idealistic, exemplifying some of the most prized of human traits. Because of this you may repress, quite ruthlessly, anything you consider unworthy. However, 'nothing dies that is not lived out' and many Aquarians are a prey to the very 'faults' you most despise, simply because you do not have the emotional honesty to face up to them and deal with them.

Feeling something is a far cry from acting upon it, but the difference may not be appreciated by you who may, instead, put a lot of energy into convincing yourself you are 'not as the rest of humanity' because you just cannot *bear* the fact you may be . . . dare we say it . . . envious, resentful, jealous, tyrannical, and hypocritical.

Before every Aquarius reading this throws down the book in disgust let me stress that most Aquarians genuinely do their best to be the best possible, at all times. What you may need to learn is that if you are able to admit to certain feelings, a) you will be far less likely to display these traits unconsciously, and b) you have far more hope of achieving genuine control and self-healing. Aquarians can be fine examples of humanity, but you are still human beings. Aquarius is a sign that is intensely proud of its humanity, and our 'flaws' are what make us human. Let's take hypocrisy first.

We have seen that Aquarius like to be thought well of in areas that are of importance. One of these is truthfulness. Now none of us can be truthful all the time and while honesty is generally the best policy there are times when life seems to steer us into lying. Like all of us, the Water Bearer can bend the truth – unconventional Aquarians are quite capable of interpreting the rules according to their own advantage. But to be called a liar, cheat, dishonest – that is more than many Aquarians can bear.

And what about tyranny? Aquarius marches under the banner of freedom – freedom of the individual, freedom for all to think and behave as they want, freedom of worship, free love, political freedom – and if others don't agree, why then they must be made to. This usually means that dissenters are not listened to or are interrupted abruptly when they try to suggest that perhaps freedom for all isn't always practical, that one person's freedom is another's bondage. This may be unwelcome stuff to the Aquarian ear, and if you can't argue them out of it, you may well walk out on them. The concept of freedom doesn't extend to those who disagree. More reasonable Aquarians are still sometimes given to making pronouncements on matters of principles that leave little freedom for others' viewpoints or feelings.

Feelings! Now there's another area. Freedom is wonderful, but not for feelings. They are better muzzled and chained like the rabid beasts they are. So if an Aquarius upsets a partner by talking to the interesting newcomer all night at the party or forgets to get a birthday card, is the partner free to be upset? Probably not. How could the partner be so uncivilised, emotional, irrational? Aquarius will leave, until the partner has calmed down and is prepared to see reason. As for the Aquarian feelings – we have already seen that these are rarely free at all. Contrary to appearances, Aquarius can be jealous, for instance. However, you are most unlikely to admit this to yourself and may well punish a partner unconsciously by withdrawing, or flirting with someone else.

You are no worse than the rest of us in respect of traditional vices, and many Aquarians are much better. Where you come unstuck is in pretending otherwise, and in behaving, in some situations, as if principles and ideals were more important than people. Ideals are to serve people as well as express the highest flowering of humanity. Emotions are what distinguish us from machines, giving rise to enduring forms of art and providing us with a surprising source of power, to the initiated. Courageous Aquarians explore this territory, also.

■ AND THE TRUTH SHALL SET YOU FREE

We know how Aquarius prizes truth, and the nature of truth is one of the Water Bearer's quests. Progressive, radical and analytical, you are often sharply perceptive: a telescope and a microscope rolled into one! You think, *really* think; you use your mind in a way that may be envied by all those with cluttered heads and preconceptions. Truth can be many things: one writer put it this way 'Truth wears many masks in order for us not to mistake appearances for reality'. Aquarius looks behind the mask and is often aware that the truth is a cube – you can see it, perhaps, but not all sides at once. What is of greatest importance is to find one's own truth – this may not be truth as seen by others, but it is a personal beacon. All Aquarians need this and most are seeking it at some level, from the most deep-thinking philosopher to the mother bringing up children and trying to shop for the family in the best way possible. As one Aquarius friend put it to me 'There are no more gurus – we all have to find our own way'. A truly Aquarian sentiment!

Ouranos and Saturn

The tale of the sky-father, Ouranos (the Greek name for Uranus), and his son, Saturn, has relevance for Capricorn as well as Aquarius. However, there are aspects to the story that are quintessentially Aquarian. Here is my version.

The ancient sky-god Ouranos was consort to Gaia, the Earth Mother, and because Gaia was so fertile they had many wondrous and monstrous offspring. None of these pleased the eye of their idealistic father, and so he pushed each and every one of his children back into their mother's womb, so he would not have to look upon their ugliness. Naturally, this made Gaia very uncomfortable and she grew gradually more and more angry, so that the very Earth groaned and rumbled with her suffering. Deciding enough was enough, she enlisted the help of one of her sons, Saturn, and furnished him with a sharp sickle, in order to take revenge upon his father.

As the Sun went down and shadows stole over the land, Ouranos descended in the night sky, to lie with his wife. But Saturn lay in wait for him in a cave on a mountain top, and at the key moment he sliced off his father's exposed genitals. As Ouranos fell back, bleeding to death, his genitals fell into the sea and the lovely goddess of lust and love, Aphrodite, was born of the foam. Where his blood dripped to

Earth, the Furies came to life. Saturn then took over his father's kingdom, but he did not keep his bargain with Gaia, which was to release her other children – so, in time, he too met his end at the hands of his own son, Zeus; but that is another story.

For Aquarius the most telling metaphor is perhaps the rejection of Ouranos's children. So many Aquarians shun what is born of the Earth, meaning what is part-and-parcel of their own humanity. This may be their own loves and hates, or it may be the practical application of their principles, which inevitably involves some compromise. It is also a metaphor for the fruits of current 'progress' – where we live ever more comfortably, travel faster, enjoy variety and convenience in clothes and food, shoving back into the earth the polluting products of our 'progress' from which they will one day, no doubt, emerge to threaten us, as Saturn did Ouranos. Modern life is to some extent a product of the Aquarian/Uranian approach, as also the attempts to reform this outlook, to espouse conservationist projects and peace initiatives.

On a personal level, idealistic Aquarians need to be aware that what they repress may 'castrate' them at some level, and that all the Furies may be let loose in their lives as a result. By the same token, what has been despised can be a source of all that is lovely and pleasurable - Aphrodite. Aquarian dreams deserve to be given fair trial in the real world, not abandoned when they prove imperfect and shoved back underground because they don't quite measure up, leaving Aquarius free to disappear into the ether once more. Not a lot can be achieved up there! Saturnian Aquarians, doing their 'duty', may need a reminder that lip service will not suffice, and that the real duty may be to face up to what lies hidden in the caves and crevices of the personality – chances are it's not nearly as bad as feared. In fact, there may be things of great beauty waiting there.

■ PRACTICE AND CHANGE ■

- You may be aware of being 'full of feeling' and may regard yourself as an emotional person – but are you *really* honest with yourself about how you feel? The territory within you is the 'undiscovered country'. What a fascinating place! Go there!

- Remember, the human race is made up of individual humans. Knowing something isn't always the same as perceiving it as a reality, at a deep level. Think about it.

- You don't have to be a paragon of perfection. Repeat three times, at regular intervals.

- I am sure that you do like the limelight at times. And why not – you deserve it. Take centre stage gracefully, when you have something to say. After all, everyone has the right to your opinion!

- Set out a freedom charter for your emotions. It is okay to feel any emotion – you may choose not to act upon it, or even express it to another person. But how can true change take place in what is repressed?

- Any reforms you plan or any new ideas you have will be far better received if you take the feelings of recipients into consideration and modify your requirements a little.

- It is truly said by the philosophers that change is the only constant. However, change for change's sake is pointless, and being different for the sake of it is an empty gesture. If you ever get caught in this, redirect your energies.

- If you are a duty-bound Aquarius, isn't it time you got a life? Unleash the occasional thunderbolt, why don't you?

2 Relationships

Try thinking of love, or something.
Amor vincit insomnia

Christopher Fry, *A Sleep of Prisoners*

I could not love thee, Dear, so much
Loved I not Honour more

Richard Lovelace, *To Lucasta, Going to the Wars*

Committed relationships present Aquarius with many conundrums. The Water Bearer combines a general love of the human race with a preoccupation for remaining apart from it that amounts to an obsession, in some individuals. Aquarius loves to be a friend, and in a sense 'loves everyone'. 'All you need is love' is the Aquarian anthem, but when it comes to personal love – the sort of love that involves self-exposure and expression of feelings – well, Aquarius would rather have a cup of tea and stare at the aspidistra.

What is it that keeps Aquarius at a distance? Two things, principally. One is the cerebral orientation of the sign and the true need for freedom of the thinking individualist and reformer. You just can't be billing and cooing if you're going to save the world, and here it may be a question of simple priorities. Fair enough. However, even saviours need a day off, so why is it that you can't get deeply involved even in your spare time? Mostly we're back with that Aquarian difficulty with emotions – scary, unreliable and chaotic as they are. This sign fears loss of control and immersion in feelings, with some justification, for you cannot function well if your logical processes are disrupted. Nonetheless, many Aquarians do succeed in making loyal and supportive partners. Hard though it may be for you to tell your love, and even harder to expose your tender spots, for many Aquarians the loved one is indescribably precious.

This intelligent and sophisticated individual may be a complete child when it comes to matters of the heart. Many run from love, until it leaps out and grabs them – then they may be helpless in its clutches and make fools of themselves. In other Aquarians standards may be more flexible than partners can handle. Many fight their feelings, intent on proving they aren't compelling, and in so doing may hurt a loved one deeply. Many Aquarians – especially the men – spend too much time working out what they think they feel, what they think they ought to feel and what they think their partner feels. This sign loves to know and analyse the feelings of others but you may keep your own very close to your chest. Attempts at empathy can be ponderous.

One of the secrets in Aquarian relationship struggles is that you don't love yourself – at least not all of yourself. You can accept only what is noble, righteous and fair. Thus, it is hard to love and relate to the more basic sides of other people without patronising, reforming and detaching. However, Aquarians are often magnetically attractive and many earnestly try, with all the dedicated idealism of which they are capable, to be good partners. The more 'Saturnine' Aquarians can apply themselves to mortgages and family commitments with realism. An Aquarius in love can be counted upon until hell freezes over, but not for empathy. Best look elsewhere for that.

■ AQUARIAN SEXUALITY

This can be complex and contradictory. Some Aquarians can genuinely take or leave sex and may choose, in the end, to do the latter as it is less troublesome. Others *say* they can do without it, but they may look a bit pinched at the corners of the mouth. These Aquarians may be coping with the frustrations of an unrewarding partnership by doing their 'duty' and telling themselves it isn't needed. Others are flagrantly promiscuous, but this may have nothing to do with a strong sex drive – some Aquarians progress from a hectic youth to a celibate middle age – and much more to do with experimentation and 'I don't see why I shouldn't'. Unless there are powerful chart factors that indicate physical drive and emotional need, Aquarius is not a passionate or highly sexed sign.

You Aquarians are often unorthodox and more able than any other sign to enjoy sex without love – or even without much feeling of any kind. You can be adept lovers, but this may have a robotic tinge and if your partner reacts in an unexpected fashion you may be nonplussed – 'I am not programmed to cover this contingency.' There is a puritanical streak in some Aquarians that may manifest as an unwillingness to reveal your nakedness, and this can have a truly touching quality, for it is as if your feelings are also on display when you take your clothes off. This can be observed in the more 'innocent' of the sign – practised lovers put up a smoother front, but even they can be put off if they think they are supposed to feel something they don't – or think they don't. This can give rise to impotence or frigidity. Many Aquarians do like erotica and are more readily turned on by a sexy idea or remark than by nudity.

Female Aquarians may project an 'ice maiden' image that is very seductive. Sometimes underneath all the ice is a tender princess, sometimes it's just ice. Ms Aquarius may be emotionally vulnerable, and thus determined to remain aloof. Theoretically she may be broad-minded, but she may also be fearful – 'I can do what I want and I don't mind if I do, but I think I'd rather I didn't.' She may defend at length the right of herself and any other woman to have sex with whom she likes, and she is sincere in this, but when it comes to the clinch she can be evasive. She's not a tease – she genuinely wants to be friendly and she finds it easy to get close to men in a platonic sense. And it is important to her to keep her freedom. But sex for her is a delicate matter. She wants to be respected, first and foremost, to have her mind valued and not to be confined. If she's promiscuous, chances are that's another form of self-protection against intimacy.

Some male Aquarians may do without sex for long periods, while for others variety is the spice of life. Mr Aquarius has probably read all the sex manuals. He may be knowledgeable and experienced, but he finds it hard to 'let go' and to enter into a powerful and overwhelming union with his partner. He likes to retain a measure of control at all times. Instinctive response to his partner may be hard for him, yet he is considerate, gentle and often open-minded – and his detachment may be provocative. Quirky things may turn him on, but the usual black-stockings-and-suspenders work for him as for the next man. Usually he prefers the strategically clad body.

You can seem so clever and worldly-wise that it may be hard to appreciate just how out of touch you may be with some basic human traits. You need to be treated with patience and sensitivity, and you perform best when least is demanded.

Merlin and Nimue

In many ways Merlin, the magician of King Arthur's court, is an Aquarian figure. Wise and detached, he stood apart from the passions and dramas of the round table. Manipulator of the royal bloodline, keen student of human nature, he traded the fulfilment of ordinary life for power. Merlin was truly wise, for he did not seek power for himself – his was 'power to' not 'power over'. Yet Merlin had needs, and these surfaced in his old age. Here is my account.

Slender as a birch, with her maidenly innocence and her woman's wit, Nimue came to the court of King Arthur to study the ways of the ageing magician, Merlin. Many feared the white-bearded old man, but not Nimue, for she had magic of her own: female magic. She watched the old enchanter from a distance and learned much while being told nothing. Merlin observed her, and turned his back, but her eyes burned into his soul.

One night when the full Moon reigned over a castle of silver and shadows, Nimue stole to Merlin's chamber and lay down beside him upon the bed. Feeling her soft presence, and believing himself to be dreaming, Merlin muttered 'Ah, Nimue, might I at last reach out and hold to me that for which I yearn – or is it too late? Love and power – is it possible to have both?'

'Ah, my dear lord,' she whispered, nestling warm against his arm, 'all things are possible. Just tell it to me, and you will see.'

Softly, from his half-slumber, Merlin spoke the words of power. Slowly and sonorously Nimue repeated them. Now a mist rose, enveloping the castle in a white gauze. Nimue took the hand of Merlin and he stood up, as one sleepwalking. Gently she led him out of the room, along the hallway and down the wide, castle steps out on to the wide moor. They came to rest by an ancient standing stone.

Now Nimue began again to speak, but the words were different this time, more commanding and strident. Around them the mist swirled, the earth on either side of the prone body of Merlin parted and gradually he was absorbed into the pearly turf. The great stone moved and came to rest over Merlin.

At length Nimue moved slowly back to the castle. It was the beginning of her reign. As for Merlin, legend says that he will awaken once more, along with his King, the 'once and future monarch' when a new age of freedom dawns and Arthur and his knights again ride forth upon the land.

We can read into this tale many things. Is it simply a story of the fate of one who bottled up his feelings all his life until, like an evil genie, they escaped and delivered him into the hands of the wrong person? Possibly. That could be an Aquarian fate, for feelings that are denied may eventually alight on someone most unsuitable, or unavailable. The metaphor of being buried under stone may also be apt. The power of the non-rational 'feminine' to beguile and bewitch is also highlighted – something which Aquarius may fear and long for. And yet is Nimue also an Aquarius? Does she sacrifice her desires, bury them 'under stone' in order to maintain control? And is this simply a tale of the acquiescence to fate by those who know it and accept it? And what of Merlin and Nimue in the 'new age' when the Sun rises on a land of freedom and promise? Perhaps the real freedom will then be the ability both to revel in the 'divine' gifts of passion and human love as well as to pursue and build an ideal of a perfect society. An impossibility? Maybe. With Aquarius, miracles take a little longer . . . .

■ AQUARIUS WOMAN IN LOVE

Ms Aquarius usually has a much better idea of how she really feels than her male counterpart. Sometimes she will spend considerable time thinking about how she feels and what she should do about it – and how she can best cope with these feelings, or whether to act upon them. She can be fiercely possessive and jealous – Aquarians don't like change, and she may feel insecure – however, she will do her best to conceal this. She is quite capable of sacrificing her real desires, rather than being 'selfish', of which she may have a horror. This can mean she renounces 'true love' for the sake of duty. It also means she may give up personal goals and preferences in favour of those of her partner. This may not be a good idea, for Ms Aquarius has a fine mind and an essentially enterprising spirit, and if these are denied she may, in time, become rigid and a little neurotic.

This lady has a generous dollop of common sense to modify her idealism. If she is in love, she rarely goes 'overboard', unless she is very young and/or impulsive, in which case it is not so much her emotions that overtake her as her desire to experiment and experience. Flirtatious, lively and intriguing, she can be a jealous man's nightmare, for she hates to be tied down, and yet she is paradoxically trustworthy: if she gives her word she means it. Don't make her feel guilty, for that will strangle her, and although it may work, in some ways it can turn your fascinating Aquarius into a martinet. She will work hard for her relationship but she needs to keep a part of herself discrete. However deeply she loves, she needs to keep a section of her mind and her life very much her own.

Ms Aquarius isn't a pushover for broad shoulders and a husky voice. Yes, she will appreciate these as much as the next girl, and may talk graphically about delicious shivers running down her spine. However, when push comes to shove she responds more deeply to intelligent and witty conversation and a man who can keep her interested. She doesn't like to be bored. Fish and peas on Friday, roast beef on Sunday, shepherd's pie on Monday are anathema to her soul, and unless she's the very Saturine Aquarian she will leap on the nearest hot air balloon rather than submit to such a routine. Because of her (perhaps secret) need to be independent, Ms Aquarius often falls for men who are unreliable or unavailable. Some Aquarian ladies can be bohemian, whereas others seem fairly conventional. However, it should never be presumed that here is a 'little woman'. She feels passionately about the position of women and would, no doubt, have chained herself to the railings along with Emmeline Pankhurst and Co had she been around at the time.

On the surface she seems to understand men well, for there is a 'masculine' side to her nature that is strong and self-sufficient. However, inside her there is a little girl, who never played with dolls and felt lonely and misunderstood when no one wanted to accompany her on her adventures or seemed interested in her chemistry set. Yes, she's truly feminine and enigmatic, quite the Snow Queen, aloof and alluring by turns. Her lovers should love Ms Aquarius without demands, learn truly to appreciate her individualism, take an interest in her projects and make her laugh – or at least take her somewhere she will find something to laugh at. Seek first a marriage of true minds' and a man will discover her true heart.

AQUARIUS MAN IN LOVE

If a woman deeply in love with an Aquarius is cut to shreds by the fact he generally ignores her and is brusque, even rude, when he just has to speak to her; if he always seems preoccupied with something else when she's around, never meets her eye and always seems much more interested in everyone else, then she should dry her eyes and take heart. She can bet her sweet life he's well and truly hooked! Mr Aquarius loves everyone – his next door neighbour, the local vagrant and the tax collector – because he should, you know. If he's not nice to her then there's a 99 per cent chance that his emotions are giving him trouble (i.e. this is 'real' love, and he's nonplussed, unsettled, scared to death).

She shouldn't expect anyone to tell her where to go from here, because this guy's an enigma, and what works for one Aquarius doesn't work for all, and anyway if it works today it won't necessarily work tomorrow. However, I can give a few pointers regarding what *not* to do. Aquarius is a victim of the Gorgon syndrome. Too much emotion, his own or anyone else's, and he turns to stone quicker than you can say 'Medusa'. Too much overt sexuality may have the same effect, for he doesn't want his hormones rampaging in public. No one, and I mean *no one* – not even a schoolgirl confronted by her favourite screen hero – blushes like an Aquarian male. Yes, his lover can wear her hemline up to her armpits and her see-through blouse, and he will defend to the death her right to wear them, as a matter of principle, naturally. Of course, he will take a sneaky look or two, but she shouldn't drape herself over him in public. Give him space to breathe and to escape from himself at regular intervals. She has to understand there is only so much this man can take.

Mr Aquarius is capable of giving his heart with the helpless devotion of a puppy. A 'safe' relationship with little passion, and duty rules, OK? To this Aquarius, once committed means 'til death us do part, because the guilt of making an ending would be a kind of death to him. Equally, Mr Saturn can give an enduring love, if the 'right' woman turns up before he acquires mortgage and manacles with the 'wrong' one. He can be tied to a dependent partner because it suits his own needs to be the strong and capable one in relationships. The male Aquarius has an even greater horror of being ignoble than his female counterpart, and will go to great lengths to convince himself that he feels what he 'should' feel. Jealousy may be the greatest monster of all, and unconsciously Mr Aquarius may take up arms and cut his own guts to shreds rather than admit he's jealous. If he has agreed on an 'open' relationship he will even drive his partner to assignations and drop her at the other fellow's doorstep, rather than submit to the tiniest bit of possessiveness. (On the other hand, an Aquarius whose secret passions are not engaged will not be slow to spot the advantages in such an arrangement!)

This is rarely a demonstrative man, and it's no good trying to make him jealous to get a reaction. It will drive him further away (as he struggles to keep his feelings at bay) and he may unconsciously punish you by flirting with someone else. He is actually as deeply, ravenously possessive as any Scorpio and just as resistant to change, but you'll have to take the word of the astrologer on that, unless you're an emotional telepath. Occasionally this progressive male can be the classical chauvinist who keeps his partner under lock and key while playing the field himself, but it is much more likely that he will religiously accord his partner total independence. Some Aquarians perpetuate their own myth of detachment and unreliability, for they like to be seen as free spirits. The inner feelings may belie this.

The best approach towards Mr Aquarius is the old 'play it cool'. He loves a woman with a lively mind and many interests: so much the better if she has original ideas of her own, he won't have to agree with them to respect them. He can be put at ease by intelligent conversation and may even relax enough to drop his eyes to the cleavage, once in a blue Uranus. It may be hard to believe it, but this man can be utterly overwhelmed by love. He may be detached, urbane, eccentric, very clever and utterly unpredictable, but his heart is like a wild bird. Keep the windows open, walk quietly, provide a little warmth and shelter and plenty of freedom, and before long you may have him eating out of your hand!

▌ GAY AQUARIUS

Some astrologers assert that Aquarius is more likely to entertain homosexual or bisexual relationships than many of the other signs – remember, these are iconoclasts, open to everything. If Aquarians experience an attraction to members of their own sex they are unlikely to be shackled by convention, or 'what the neighbours think'. Aquarians are sometimes quite capable of experimenting with homosexual love just to see what it's like, how it feels. Certainly they are likely to be utterly tolerant of the sexual proclivities of others and may enjoy keeping company with cross-dressers and 'out' couples, because they are different, interesting people with extensive experience of life. Most Aquarians would say that sexual orientation doesn't matter, and in this they are most refreshing.

■ AQUARIUS LOVE TRAPS

Duty bound

Here we are recapping on one of the themes outlined above – that compulsion in many Aquarians to 'do the right thing'. Because your sign is so idealistic and so estranged from your own emotional side, you can be the most strong-principled of all. Of course, this may seem like a great virtue (Aquarius certainly believes so!) but it stems to a great extent from a lack of realism about human relationships – for fulfilment is not found through suppression. It is also due, in no small measure, to the trouble the Water Bearer has with emotions, and it is far safer to stick with what is emotionally undemanding, and not to face the heartache and recriminations of a split. It may seem hard to understand that this sign, which is so unconventional and original could possibly submit to such a bondage, but this is *emotional* bondage, not political or ideological.

If you are an Aquarius who has trouble allowing yourself emotional freedom you may like to approach this situation from another angle. Isn't your continuation in a dead relationship an insult to the other party? Does he or she not have the right to find someone who will give what is needed, not just pretend to? Is either of you really happy? Of course, the ability to ask yourself these questions presupposes a degree of emotional honesty, anyway, and that is half the battle. How can the spirits of either of you be free under these circumstances? And are you hooked on having someone who depends on you, in preference to having to look certain facts about yourself in the face, such as your own secret dependency issues, or the need to prove that you are 'above it all'? If you have the courage to ask such things then you can pat yourself on the back. If the answers are less than satisfactory, then why not take hold of the matter in a truly civilised way, with a view to sorting it out?

Forbidden fruit

While the more 'saturnian' Aquarian may be more prone to the 'duty bound' trap (though the 'Uranian' are by no means immune) 'forbidden fruit' applies mostly to the more unconventional side of Aquarius. This can mean that you are drawn to relationships with partners of other people, or to those who are otherwise unavailable, to people of widely differing cultural backgrounds, large age gaps, and also to all types of 'kinky sex' or just to a life of relentless, promiscuous experimentation. All this can sound like fun, and indeed for many it can *be* fun, if proper precautions are taken. However, it may in the end leave a rather dry taste in the mouth. For underneath all the adventure may lurk that old fear of intimacy. Of course, because you often flout convention you are more likely to be open to unusual relationships, and many make a success of such arrangements. Also it is a mistake to state that you need intimacy and must find some way of achieving it to be half-fulfilled, for Aquarius also needs other things, such as genuine freedom, mental stimulation and ideals for which to aim. But if you are going to undertake relationships at all then it is worthwhile looking at the dynamics. Most of us do want to be close to another human being, to find a partner, and few people – even Aquarians – are likely to find a soulmate via bondage and black rubber. If this is you, do you need to ask yourself what you are running from? Is this all as exciting as it ought to be?

◼ AQUARIUS AND MARRIAGE

This sign of the iconoclast often avoids legal marriage as being unnecessary, or somehow debasing. Why should two noble souls need this 'bit of paper'? Aquarius may decide not to get married in order to prove a political point. Aquarians may also develop long-term relationships with foreigners, sometimes where there is a significant language barrier. There may be immense difference in ages. This sign is likely to try domestic set-ups that are far from run of the mill, such as sharing a house with several other couples, living in a commune or reversing stereotyped roles so the male stays at home and brings up the children. Aquarius, especially the more 'Uranian', doesn't marry for practical reasons, or for social accept-ability. Shared ideals are likely to be of paramount importance to you. Some Aquarians are very shy of marriage and hold up impossi-ble criteria that have to be fulfilled before they will tie any knot. Others simply never give up their independence, or even muster enough interest in the whole subject to get anywhere near the altar. However, those Aquarians who do plump for commitment try hard to fulfil their responsibilities and are often faithful, if for no better reason than they are only too pleased not to have to waste time chasing around, and can concentrate on building the radio tele-scope in the shed, or running for the local elections. Yours is an earnest and well-meaning sign and while your attention may often be absent, if you have given your word it means you keep it.

■ WHEN LOVE WALKS OUT – HOW AQUARIUS COPES

It may come as a terrible shock to Aquarius to come home and find the bird has flown, but it happens all too often, because the Water Bearer is deaf and blind when it comes to emotional signals, and sometimes apparently deaf to outright pleas and tears, too. The part-ners of Aquarians may feel misunderstood and alone for a long time, while Aquarius blissfully spends every spare moment bird watching or raising money for the orphans of Brazil. Crying on the shoulder of a 'friend' can turn into something much more, on the basis that Aquarius won't listen anyway; and the truth is that sometimes it is only when the partner walks out that Aquarius has a clue that anything is wrong, and then it is usually too late.

Aquarius may then become a little eccentric, ever more absorbed in pursuits and even more estranged from true feelings. You can be deeply hurt, and you do not recover quickly. Repressed anger may also rankle, especially if the relationship was one that you had 'dutifully' endured. This can make you decide not to try again – ever. Needless to say, this is not a decision to be taken because of disappointment and sour grapes. You Aquarians need plenty of time to explore yourselves and ask what went wrong – yes, yet another plea for emotional honesty. You should try not to disappear inside yourself, but may instead devote time to pursuits the matter to you, not in order to escape from feelings but to give scope to life to open up and find meaning.

Starting afresh

This sign of the revolutionary may take a long time to make successful internal shifts, but if there has been a failure of a significant relationship, that may be exactly what is required. You may adhere rigidly to your ideas and may find it very hard to see what went wrong; you may be all too prone to dismiss the break-up as some sort of mental aberration on the partner's side. Of course, all of us are subject to relationship problems and it is rare indeed to encounter someone who hasn't been through it all, at some point. Not all relationships are built to last, and that's a fact. However, where issues are unclear, problematic or plain surprising to you, some real thinking needs to be undertaken in order to make some sort of change. This isn't just a matter of labelling what has happened in the manner beloved of the logical mind: it may mean a radical and sometimes painful change. It is then important for you to come to some idea of what you want/need from a future partnership, if any. Meanwhile Aquarius is usually a sign of many interests, many friends, and this can be a valuable interlude to devote to extending some of these.

■ PRACTICE AND CHANGE ■

- Yours can be a proud sign, and admitting there is an area you struggle with, particularly emotions, is not always easy for you. It can mean a lot to partners if you can say 'I'm really sorry, but I struggle with this'.

- Do remember to tell your loved one how precious he or she is to you.

- The feelings of others may be fascinating, but restrain yourself from over-analysing and assuming you understand how they feel – chances are you don't.

- Try to accept and embrace all parts of yourself, even those you regard as unworthy and embarrassing. This will make you a more complete human being.

- Emotions do not always have to be labelled and talked about. Emotions are about saying how you feel, not necessarily why, or making any sense of the whole thing at all. Try to understand what your partner is really feeling rather than quoting one of your ideas.

- Remember, love can only enlarge you, in the end, and it will not deprive you of power over yourself.

- Don't kid yourself that bottled-up feelings will disappear. Energy is never destroyed, only changed, and what is repressed cannot transform. If you want to make real changes those feelings have to be expressed in some form. That doesn't mean that we all are enslaved by our impulses, but it does mean that we acknowledge them as real and meaningful forces within us.

3 All in the family

Piping down the valleys wild
Piping songs of pleasant glee
On a cloud I saw a child . . .

William Blake, *Song of Innocence, Introduction*

Having an Aquarius in the family can be like living in a mine field, or with an angel – or with no one at all. These are unpredictable souls, interested in everything from interstellar travel to the contemplation of their own navel. Some Aquarians are so absent-minded that the house may be perpetually booby trapped by their scattered belongings. Others are much more controlled, and their cultured disposition makes them pleasant and helpful family members. You can never be quite sure just what they will do, however, so don't be surprised if you come home to find the Mad Hatter having tea in your kitchen . . . .

■ AQUARIUS MOTHER

Ms Aquarius is never quite sure if motherhood is for her, and she still hasn't made up her mind as she counts the stars with her third grandchild. Let's face it, children are such a tie. They bring one's mind down from the ether and into nappies and routines. However, they can also be endless fun – there's always something new with a child, always something to tease the brain, and Aquarius can enjoy the adventure of life with little ones – after that first, leaky stage is passed.

Aquarius mother may alternate between endless theorising and a laid-back attitude. Her worries may nag at her: she may be a whizz at atomic physics, or have written three bestsellers, but she still doesn't really understand the ordinary world and why the neighbours object to her old caravan parked on the drive. Although she has learnt to get along with everyone and may say and do the right things, she is still uneasy at letting loose her little one in this perplexing environment. Often she has avant-garde ideas and may educate her children at home or think nothing of them running around the garden at midnight. She is rarely overly protective, but she will listen patiently and fairly to all grievances and problems. She often has the gift of making her children laugh, seeing the absurdity in it all. Aquarius mother has that wonderful ability to recede to a bird's eye view, where all pretty wranglings assume correct proportion – i.e. minuscule. And she can take her children with her on this magical flight.

This is not the most demonstrative mother: she isn't a great one for cuddles, she would rather talk. She comes into her own when her children at last reach school age and there is homework to help them with, and a PTA to join. She may be the most active mum at the school fête. Generally her views are open and unprejudiced. Hers is an open house, and her children's friends are likely to flock to her door with tales of woe and sexual experimentation that they would never discuss with their own parents. Aquarius mother is likely to take her young daughter to the Family Planning clinic herself rather than ignore her daughter's burgeoning sexuality. She is usually modern and free thinking (although some Aquarians can be very strict and unbending), but it may sometimes feel hard to get close to her and she may well analyse her children's problems rather than giving them sympathy.

Aquarius mother is likely to cook in a microwave and eat picnic-style in front of the latest Sci-Fi video, discussing with her children how the plot could have been improved. She expands boundaries and is usually a stimulating companion: she would rather be a 'best mate' than a mum. However, she is likely to instil high principles and an ability in her children to think for themselves – after all, she always does. Children should treasure Aquarius mum, never buy her soppy ornaments or mugs that bear the legend 'Best Mum in the World'. Rather they should buy her a tee-shirt from Greenpeace, with endangered species on the front – she feels like one of those at times. and pay her the ultimate compliment: always tell her the truth. She can take it.

■ AQUARIUS FATHER

At his best this guy's a real box of tricks, so his kids feel like the Sorceror's Apprentice. He's usually doing something fascinating, whether it's breeding owls at the bottom of the garden or building a time machine in the woodshed. Of course, he may elevate the term 'absent father' to new levels – absent even when present, and that only infrequently – but he is far more likely to take parenthood as a serious trust, and to enjoy it, up to a point.

Aquarius dad may relate brilliantly to the troubles of children, for they are generally simple and easy to fix, and they don't drag at his entrails the way adult problems may do. Dolly's arm can be stuck back on and Hayley's tears can be dried on dad's torn sleeve, while he looks out for a dandelion clock to blow the time. As for Red Riding Hood and that wolf, dad can never understand how she could possibly have been so mistaken. Wolves don't look a bit like Grannies, do they? Perhaps she had dust in her eye from all that walking, or perhaps Granny had a bristly chin like old Mrs Paterson down at the Post Office – to Aquarius dad there's always a story within a story within a story and he's ready to ask that magic word 'Why' along with his children, and to help them find an answer.

Like his feminine counterpart, he's a great pal. He knows where the badgers live, and will organise a midnight expedition to watch them come out. He's more familiar with the local recycling programme than he is with the geography of the kitchen, but it can be rewarding to help him find where mum put the tea bags. He may well enlist the help of his children in campaigning for equality for ethnic minorities, and when he goes out for a walk in his faded brown cords and shirt from Oxfam his family may walk ten paces ahead! Sometimes it does seem as if he cares more about the homeless than about his own leaking roof, and it might seem as if equality applies to everyone but his family. However, parochial he is not. As long as he isn't too cranky to relate, he can give his children the gift of a panoramic view that is exciting and gives them a true sense of responsibility and world citizenship.

Most Aquarius fathers are liberal and tolerant, but there are the occasional martinets who may shout from the soapbox about 'Gay Liberation' but keep their families under virtual house arrest. This can arise from the impulse within some Aquarians to be controlling; this is a Fixed sign, and freedom may be a fervent ideal, while the reality is much less elastic. Aquarius can also be stern and quite unrealistically high minded. This sort of Aquarian may be a stringent disciplinarian, with never a hint of the whimsical – but such are a comparative rarity. Much more likely this is a father who will throw open house for your bohemian friends and cook veggie-burgers on the barbecue (or rather burn them, while he catches up with the latest edition of the *Big Issue*). He doesn't poo-pooh any crazy idea – he develops it. He wants his children to be thinking, responsible and reformative members of society, and he gives them a jet-propelled start.

■ THE AQUARIUS CHILD

Is this an infant prodigy, or a headless chicken headed straight for the Funny Farm? You may not be sure, but the neighbours are likely to have some pretty set views on the subject, when Aquarius's kite tangles with their television aerial, or the fire service arrives *again* 'because the Bunsen burner fell over and meths readily ignites, and the curtains – well, there wouldn't be curtains in a proper laboratory, now, would there?'

Curiosity killed the cat, but it may seem like young Aquarius has the nine feline lives. However, will the cat survive? Only with luck, after Aquarius has tied helium balloons to all four legs, and tail – purely in the interests of science, of course. Strongly Aquarian children can be negative, contrary and incomprehensible: 'yes' may be the last word they learn as they live on dry cornflakes and become welded to a tee-shirt they've slept, eaten and played in for three days. They can be a parent's nightmare, especially a very controlling parent, who likes to see each pea consumed in an orderly fashion. However, force Aquarius into a straight-jacket of 'Be like little Billy down the road' and you may well turn this youngster really cranky, instead of just whacky. Aquarius sees life with clear eyes, and it is wise parents who asks themselves 'What does it *really* matter?' Probably it doesn't, and Aquarius has spotted that fact. These kids can teach a parent a thing or two.

Of course, not all Aquarians are variations on the theme of *Young Einstein*. Some are sweet and whimsical, but the still possess a grain of the unpredictable. The broad sweep of their gaze can take in the fact that society expects certain things, and while no Aquarius is without a touch of individualism, many of these children are polite and considerate – this is a civilised sign, and one that likes to 'do the right thing', remember? However, manners will rarely prevent them from asking telling questions and persisting until they get a truthful answer. A three-year-old Aquarius may have to be rushed out of the shop, because the strident 'Mum, *why* is that lady so fat?' causes embarrassment, but fifteen years later many questions have received answers that have led to straight A's and a scholarship to Oxbridge. Even non-academic Aquarians are still original thinkers and need plenty of mental stimulation.

These children often dream about what life will be and have many ambitions and aspirations, that usually involve general benefit to society, as well as to themselves. It may be hard to get them off to school as their noses are buried in 'What The Time Lord Did Next' and finding their shoes may be akin to an expedition up the Amazon. Aqurians need plenty of fresh air and physical activity, so they don't disappear inside themselves. They also need a fairly equable environment, for they are almost telepathic and will pick up on undercurrents.

This is the natural 'twenty-first century' gal or guy, but adolescence may arrive almost unnoticed, as Aquarius is still preoccupied with building a radio receiver or taking the PC apart and upgrading it. Aquarius should almost always be supplied with state-of-the-art technology – the best you can afford (but *not* for disassembling – for using). Plenty of books, CD Roms, opportunity to explore and question, question, question. Some Aquarians are outdoor types and best provided with camping gear and mature companions. These intelligent youngsters are often babies in the ways of the world and may need to be reminded often not to run off alone or to talk to strangers. Aquarian girls need to be treated with especial sensitivity, because they will deeply resent it if they get the impression that their sex constrains their freedom, and may be more likely to walk the streets at midnight in their Doc Martens just to prove they can. When sexuality does hit this young person, it may be quite hard (desperate and uncommunicable love) or a complete non-event as the many friendships acquire another dimension (and the word 'experiment' acquires meanings that have nothing to do with test-tubes). If Aquarius wishes for many sexual relationships he or she is unlikely to be diverted by your arguments, so best make sure the proper precautions are in place and that all your advice is sensible and unprejudiced. Keep your moralising to yourself or you may be hit in the face with 'Well, you and Daddy did it, didn't you?'

Some Aquarians are difficult to raise, while some are model citizens almost from the start – citizens of the future. Whatever the case, your Aquarius child is unlikely to be dull. The young Aquarius brings her or his parents a great gift – that of teaching *them* something and of making them feel they have a part in time to come. After all, we do not own our children, and certainly never our Aquarians. Children are our gift to the future – what more priceless gift than an Aquarius?

■ AQUARIUS AS SIBLINGS

This brother or sister may be totally wrapped up in their own concerns or a continual liability, as their siblings' Lego gets hi-jacked to make a 'Sock Putting On Machine'. Teddy's head may be dissected 'to see if he has any brains' and the alarm clock may disappear into a mass of cogs and wheels. If Aquarius is the younger sibling it's no good pulling rank – he or she doesn't respect the authority of teachers or parents so what hope do siblings have? Also Aquarius doesn't respond well to emotional appeals.

Aquarius can be older siblings' worst nightmare come to life as they try to act cool in front of their mates, and their Aquarius brother or sister pipes up 'Why are you talking in that funny voice?' However, Aquarius can be coped with. What siblings must do is: a) always explain everything, especially things of an emotional nature, as clearly as possible; b) answer all questions with absolute frankness; c) respect the intelligence of this sister or brother. If siblings are going to put on an act or tell a lie to someone in their company, best tell Aquarius in advance, for the chances are he or she will be loyal, even if a little uncomprehending, and may begin to value an older sister or brother as someone who can teach Aquarius a thing or two about this mysterious thing called life.

■ AQUARIUS IN THE HOME

If you are short of space, the best first step is to ask your Aquarius for suggestions, for Aquarius can be extremely resourceful. On the other hand you will also be given some wild ideas about digging a cellar under the living room, or moving to the Outback – you will have to sort the wheat from the chaff. Aquarius usually does need a fair bit of space: this Air sign doesn't like to be cooped up. As it is a rare Aquarius who cares about status, a move to a shabbier, larger place might suit Aquarius, if not the rest of the family. For Aquarius it may actually be a good idea to place a small trailer on the lawn or convert the garden shed so that it offers some amenities. Aquarian kids sometimes are willing to camp out in the garden for days, so a good tent may be worthwhile – and check your garden is well fenced, to secure against entry by strangers. Most Aquarians are interested in technology and in how things work, so space to take apparatus apart, or to place the PC are more important than room to hang clothes. Aquarius is only rarely interested in personal appearance.

■ PRACTICE AND CHANGE ■

- Aquarian parents need to be careful that they are not too emotionally and physically remote. Cuddles are important. Not all problems are for solving, or diverting by laughter.

- Aquarians must realise that their children need to 'fit in' and may not always want to appear unconventional, or the first to make it to the year 2050. You respect all freedoms so respect their freedom to be one of the crowd if they choose.

- It is important for Aquarians to give their children emotional freedom as well as other freedoms. Seek to help youngsters cope with all emotions.

- Charity begins at home – many Aquarians need a reminder of this.

- Do not be too high principled. Human nature is built upon a bedrock of animal, vegetable and mineral.

- Aquarian children need to be allowed freedom to experiment, but they need also to know the value of empathy and sympathy. This is perhaps best taught by example.

- Aquarian children need freedom and scope, but they need also to learn the dangers of this less-than-perfect world.

- Never trample on Aquarian dreams, for Aquarians will merely become introverted and feel the world doesn't understand them.

- Aquarians do need a peaceful environment, especially when young. They can be disturbed by turbulent atmospheres, so they may retreat.

- With all Aquarians a democratic household works best. Everyone should have their say and undertake their share of related chores.

4 Friendship and the single life

Love is only chatter
Friends are all that matter

Gelett Burgess

Aquarian partnerships can involve a cast of thousands that includes old flames and squatters from the condemned building across town. A committed relationship doesn't in any way cool the Aquarian love affair with the human race, and partners have to learn to share their Aquarius – or perhaps join in the fun.

■ AQUARIUS AS A FRIEND

You Aquarians are friends to all, but probably really close to few, if any. You are the sort of person who will not want to commit to being just in one place, physically and mentally, for an entire evening. Rarely will you listen endlessly to friends' moans and groans – unless they're going either to take your advice, or a philosophical approach, or both, for after all, the advice is probably one and the same. You love to analyse all your friends' mental and emotional processes. Aquarians often pride themselves on being the souls of sympathy. While you can be a loyal, devoted and resourceful helper, there's only just so much of 'crying into your beer' that you can take. You like to solve the problem, take friends out of themselves and make them laugh. If you can't do this, you may leave friends alone for a while, so that they can get over it.

Aquarians do love to give advice and can occasionally be quite dictatorial. After all, you've thought it all out and you know what friends should do. If they don't agree you may be offended – although you would not put it that way. Being a dynamic friend is very important to you and your self-image. If you seem a little brusque or bossy it is because you cannot bear to 'sit' with friends' feelings – which is often all that can be done. You have to get to the bottom of it all and find an answer.

You love to have a good talk and you will thoroughly enjoy friends' company if you can spend time discussing important issues like social reform or new ways of doing just about anything. Less academic Aquarians like to go out a lot, often to fringe theatre or open-air concerts – or just to old haunts where they can meet the crowd and perhaps see a few new faces, too. Many Aquarians like to find someone or something that will make them laugh. Aquarians need to befriend the human race and his dog, and some need to make it obvious that they have many friends. However, chances are you keep all and sundry at something of a distance, for that suits you.

Aquarians are often inverted snobs. You would far rather spend time with those others might despise than hang around with the cream of society. You are a true and loyal friend. If you do not agree with friends' opinions you will nonetheless 'defend to the death' their right to hold them. If friends want an interesting discussion with someone who will really use his or her mind, you are their person. If friends want the truth they will get it from you. Friends shouldn't look to you for deep rapport, for only rarely can you manage that, although you will be there for them in times of crisis. They should not expect the reward of being able to help you, either, for Aquarius are self-sufficient people and you would rather help yourself, although you do not always take your own advice! Aquarians are great lovers of humanity, so friends can only expect to get a piece of your affection. But it can be an interesting, stimulating, shining piece that makes friends feel part of something meaningful. That's no mean gift – from a friend to a friend!

■ AQUARIUS AND THE SINGLE LIFE

Aquarians need lots of space and you are one of the signs best adapted to living without a partner. There are so many things to which you love to devote your time. Rodin's sculpture *The Thinker* is very much an Aquarian study. There may not be much room left in your life for close relating. In any case, you often like to have plenty of time alone in order to work out what is going on inside you. Often there will be many false starts and radical shifts before you are able to orientate yourself.

You do like to explore arcane, esoteric and futuristic subjects. The entire 'New Age' is your playground. Aquarians are often happy inhabiting a complex conceptual structure and behaving as if it is logically and practically proven, even when it isn't. The Water Bearer has an intuitive mind-set and can sometimes see 'cosmic patterns'. You may spend a great deal of time perfecting systems and then wonder why no one understands. However, to many people you are an inspiration – fascinating, with some intriguing mental twists and turns. Developing all this may require some solitude.

However, few of us are happy being solitary, and this Air sign is no exception. You need to communicate what you have learnt, or you may just need someone to have fun with or to stimulate you. Aquarius often meets friends through groups and societies – for that is your natural habitat. This sign is most open-minded about associates. You won't turn away because someone has the wrong clothes, or accent; you give everyone equal chance, and because of this often find valuable friendships that expand and sharpen your experience of life. Interesting and electric, you rarely have trouble striking up friendships – unless something in life has made you feel you are written off as an old eccentric. However, even in a crowd you are, in a sense, alone. Aquarius sees what others do not see, and while you may be chattering as superficially and as vivaciously as the next person, there is a part of you holding aloof. That part is probably en route for Sirius – maybe one day the rest of us will catch up!

■ PRACTICE AND CHANGE ■

- Aquarians who offer advice like crumbs to wild birds, rather than by force-feeding are liable to be the most valuable, for sooner or later a friend can return to those words of wisdom and take them up, if they are appropriate.

- Being a friend may also mean allowing yourself to be helped. Like the other Fixed signs, Aquarius doesn't like to be dependent, but paying a friend the compliment of helping you is simple psychology.

- If you are a 'dutiful', 'unselfish' Aquarian, are you taking enough time alone to explore and expand your mind? You also have a 'duty' to yourself, and you have a deep need to discover, explore, study, conceptualise and grow. Give yourself the space to be your own person, and then offer others the gift of what you have found out and the inspiration of your enthusiasm.

- Emotional rapport isn't easy for you – be honest, but your friends appreciate your simple presence.

- If you are an Aquarius who hasn't joined some sort of group of like-minded people, ask yourself if this is really okay for you. If not, go out and find one – and join this week.

5

Career

Two roads diverged in a wood, and I –
I took the one less travelled by,
And that has made all the difference

Robert Frost

Aquarius is the supreme individualist whatever niche you occupy in life. Some Aquarians find it difficult in the extreme to conform to requirements set by routine and by other people – you can usually see other, better ways of doing things. However, Aquarius is also capable of hard work and great concentration. Many Aquarians are sharply aware of their commitments and make it a point of honour never to let anyone down and to support their family with dedication.

The idealism of Aquarius if often evident in choice of career and position occupied. Equality, truth, freedom and the significance of the work itself are likely to be prized above status and money. However, Aquarians are often successful, because you have enterprise and imagination, and are usually without blinkers when it comes to making creative changes. You are rarely ambitious but your streak of genius sometimes means you have 'greatness thrust upon you'. Equally, Aquarians may work in obscurity, if you feel that what you are doing is worthwhile, or gives you the independence you crave.

◼ TRADITIONAL AQAURIUS CAREERS

The common denominator for all occupations suitable for Aquarius is that they involve variety, independence, humanitarian or scientific approach and in some cases considerable independence of action. Aquarius careers include:

- scientist
- writer
- politician
- sociologist
- social worker
- charity worker
- astrologer
- astronomer
- technician (especially TV and computers)
- radiographer
- archaeologist

- inventor
- work for humanitarian organisations such as Greenpeace, UN, etc.
- air force
- electrician
- broadcaster
- publisher
- media
- photographer
- psychologist

■ WHAT TO LOOK FOR IN YOUR WORK

Many people work in large insurance corporations, sales offices, shops, banks and factories. Only relatively few of us can choose a profession, train for it and find a fulfilling lifestyle, and as time progresses this is becoming more elusive.

To help you find a job that suits you, you need to bear in mind the spirit of what is recommended, not the specific occupation. One office job is not like another, one shop selling fashions may differ enormously from one down the street in terms of environment and opportunity. As an Aquarius you need to make sure of several things when seeking employment:

- There is as much freedom to organise your own day as possible.
- Your work involves variety and a flavour of the unexpected.
- There will be scope for you to use your initiative, make changes.
- You are not involved in anything, even obliquely, that contravenes your code of ideals. For instance, if you are against smoking, you may not be able to cope with working in a shop that sells cigarettes.

- You can find something interesting and/or meaningful in your work. For instance, you may be a cleaner. It will feel far more worthwhile to be cleaning in a children's home, hostel, hospital or such like than to be polishing tables for 'fat cats'.
- The people you work for are congenial, friendly and open.
- You are paid what you are worth.
- You can believe, somewhere in the back of your mind, that this job isn't going to go on forever, and some day, some way, you'll be walking the slopes of Kilimanjaro/running your own healing centre/not have to work at all and free to spend all your time studying or with your favourite hobby.

So there is no need to feel you have to look for a specifically Aquarian job. Many Aquarians would be bored to death by archaeology and some don't know the front of a television from the back! Look for something that suits in its content and atmosphere rather than its label. If you are sure it doesn't suit, move on. Realise that this job will not fulfil you and look elsewhere, sooner rather than later.

■ THE BOHEMIAN

This person may live in an attic, eat baked beans out of a tin while reading *The New Scientist* or '101 Things To Do With A Quartz Crystal' and go to work in clothes that look as if they've been slept in. They sit on the desk, or put their feet on it, and take their work with them into the lavatory. They are annoying, mesmerising, and probably brilliant, otherwise why would their boss tolerate them?

The Bohemian is probably friendly and may stand drinks for everyone, and there may even be an aura of illegal substances about their person. At other times this person is virtually penniless, and crouches in a corner over a small beer. Bohemian is harmless and can be inspiring – the only danger is that colleagues may rely on him or her – don't. If Bohemian offers to help, it is a sincere offer – except that time is often an irrelevance to this person.

If you're The Bohemian, and you're successful – by that I mean happy and able to find next month's rent – then you need no advice from me. On the other hand, if you are determined to flout every known convention – and some of the lesser known – and find that you are too poor to afford a new nose stud, then what are you trying to prove? Isn't your individuality and talent better expressed by making intelligent compromise, so you at least get some opportunities, rather than doors slammed in your face? Anyone can be different; isn't it more important to make a difference?

■ THE ALIEN

Employees with this Aquarian boss should hold on to their hats, and their sanity. One day they may come in to find the filing cabinets are hanging from the ceiling 'because having them in the corner is so boring'. If this is a colleague, life will be equally erratic, with nothing ever done the same way twice.

The Alien is often quite a frustrated soul whose job doesn't give enough scope. Genius *manqué*, the Alien should not be in any ordinary sphere and probably hasn't yet worked out what his or her vocation may be so that when the call comes this person will be off. Meanwhile colleagues have to cope with a cross between the Mad Professor and a neurotic robot.

Many Aquarians have at least an ingredient of the Alien – it's part of their character, and the only reason it's notable is that it sits about as comfortably as ET with what most of us are pleased to call 'normal' life. There is a part of Aquarius that really can look at everything with the detached vision of beings who have just arrived from another galaxy, and that is why they may be prepared to make changes and are chafing to spread conceptual boundaries. The Alien may make changes for the sake of them or, like Bohemian may be different, just for the sake of it. However, chances are these people really can see things that the rest of us miss.

The best thing colleagues who have to work with an Alien can do is to modify their schemes to make them workable; it might not be hard to spot the advantages in this. Many Aquarians will be aware of an 'alien' component in their personality, although in some of the more 'Saturnian' this may be harder to discern. This quality can range from a feeling of not being quite understood, not quite fitting in, to an extremely uncomfortable and frustrating sensation that results from being the only person in the room who hears the drummer. These are themes we have encountered in an earlier chapter. Aquarius can't always compromise; as Robert Frost wrote 'Something there is that doesn't love a wall, That wants it down.' However, if you demolish, others will simply rebuild. The only way forwards is gently, reasonably, bit by bit. Rome wasn't bulldozed in a day!

■ THE AQUARIUS BOSS

It may be quite surprising that this person ever made it to an executive chair, for Aquarians don't often like giving orders – although giving them may be far preferable to taking them! This is 'one of the gang' prepared to take everyone as she or he finds them, often tolerant to a fault of late comers and lax dressers. However, it would be a great mistake to challenge the authority of Aquarius bosses for while they may not pull rank, they will pull dignity, superior mentality and lightning wit.

Aquarius boss will value employees' ideas and they have every chance of seeing their innovations at least given a try. This person is fair and progressive. Just occasionally some of the less desirable traits of the Aquarian opposite, Leo, are in evidence, and some Aquarians are guilty of passing off other people's ideas as their own. The best approach with Aquarius is always to be open and honest.

Aquarius might just understand if employees admit to taking the day off yesterday because they were fed up and frustrated – as long as they've come back today renewed and determined to work hard. However, if they phone to say they have a migraine, but somebody spots them in the supermarket – Heaven help them!

This boss probably doesn't understand too well anyone's ambitions for promotion; some Aquarians don't have an ambitious bone in their body. Some others are eager only to get on so they have more independence. Aquarius generally isn't understanding about requests for a raise in salary, either. Of course, everyone should be paid what they are worth, no more and no less. Some Aquarians don't see why the canteen attendant shouldn't be paid as much as the MD: after all, both work hard, and at least the MD gets to sit down more often!

Aquarius gives employees their independence, interfering with their work, dress, time-keeping and extra-curricular activities as little as humanly possible. However, if they are asked for advice, they may be a little impatient if employees don't take it. Aquarius boss is no sucker for sob stories; sympathy will be given so far, but after that everyone has to sort out their own life. Sometimes this person appears to assume employees have invisible antennae – Aquarius can take off at a moment's notice and forget to inform anyone.

The great thing about this boss is the feeling of freedom that employees get if they only 'play the game'. Only quite rarely does the more Saturnian Aquarian become the rigid disciplinarian. If employees are straight and fair themselves it is hard to go wrong with this person. The only trouble is that, just when employees have got used to all the unpredictable ways, their Aquarian boss takes off for another corner of the galaxy, either promoted (almost in spite of themselves) or gone elsewhere, where there's more 'room to breathe'.

■ THE AQUARIUS EMPLOYEE

These people may turn up for work wearing odd shoes, and they may forget their briefcase, but their head, luckily, remains attached, and it is all the average Aquarius needs in order to work a successful and inspired day. Employers should not expect conventionality, or any kow-towing: Aquarius accords respect only where it is merited, and fancy titles and leather-topped desks leave him or her cold, even if they are noticed. Aquarius are far more likely to notice the birds nesting under the eaves, and be led by this to a brilliant new idea on insulation, or customer relations, for example.

Resourceful, and habitually 'laterally thinking' Aquarius throws off ideas like discarded chocolate wrappers. Not all are workable, but some are adaptable. Among all the glittery bits there will be the occasional flash of pure genius. Don't miss this. Aquarians are often a little aloof and they rarely push their ideas, or themselves forward: it is rather beneath their dignity. Besides, Aquarians aren't usually looking for recognition, promotion or success: other things are more important to them. Sometimes it is unclear what these things may be, even to Aquarius, and sometimes, it has to be said, Aquarius considers it most infra dig to appear to care a scrap for the approval of anyone. However, this is a conscientious and intelligent employee with a strong sense of honour and responsibility.

Aquarians are generally friendly to everyone, and while they aren't always good at PR – many are a little abrupt at times and too idealistic to spot a shady deal – they may genuinely not notice when someone is grumpy or rude, and thus can bring out the best in them. These people are not above bending the rules at times, or coming up with some surprising interpretations of them, but outright dishonesty is generally beneath them. If employers are not too touchy about their dignity or too cast-iron about routine, they will come to value their Aquarian alchemist. Don't take too long to appreciate Aquarian employees – they may not be around for long!

■ WHEN UNEMPLOYMENT STRIKES

The more Saturnian Aquarians may find unemployment a worrying state, and will use all their resourcefulness to find a job as soon as possible. Aquarians are often prepared to turn their hand to anything when necessity strikes, while the more revolutionary type of Aquarians may hardly bother about income drying up, with ultimate faith in the universe and their own powers to pull them through. There is no doubt that many Aquarians value greatly the freedom that comes with unemployment, and if there has been a trapped feeling about work, the sound of shackles falling is like music. Some Aquarians have little to lose when unemployment is forced upon them, for they don't care much for status or money and can always find something far more interesting to occupy their time. However, this isn't always true: female Aquarians are generally more practical, Aquarians with commitments will worry about reneging on them, and it is also possible that Aquarian pride can be hurt by unemployment. Loss of job can be devastating when it has been a vocation, and the life of Aquarius has been bound up in it to a great extent.

Aquarians should not try to convince themselves that they 'don't care' and are 'above all of that' when they are unemployed. They should not allow themselves to be distracted from the business of finding fresh employment by other pursuits, and they should guard against becoming erratic and ungrounded. Certain things need your attention including money, this will ultimately leave you with more genuine freedom to follow what truly matters.

■ SELF-EMPLOYMENT AND OTHER MATTERS

Not all work relies on a company and an employer, for there are many other approaches. Of all the signs of the zodiac Aquarius is the most likely to be happiest when self-employed. Independent, open-minded and imaginative, Aquarius is usually able to exploit all opportunities. This sign is not especially given to anxiety, and Aquarius do not typically crave an opulent lifestyle. Creative thinkers, inventors and entrepreneurs, Aquarians love the power that self-employment offers to direct their own lives and to move where they like. Self-employed Aquarians do need to be aware that they are not always practical and that they are often ill-tuned to the thoughts and feelings of other people. If they are prepared to modify their offbeat approach, they should find this lifestyle rewarding.

■ PRACTICE AND CHANGE ■

- In your work you should have independence, scope, variety, a sense of being meaningful and friendly companionship.
- Do not be different for the sake of it. Isn't that really beneath you? Why waste your talent?
- You do really want to make actual, creative change, but make it slowly, with due regard for the feelings of others.
- Always be honest and open with an Aquarius boss and respect independence if you are given it. Some Aquarians can be rigid, but even they may be coaxed by a new idea.
- Aquarian employees need scope and their ideas need to be appreciated. Do not waste these propensities by insisting they act like one of the paving stones.
- If you are an unemployed Aquarius, avoid denial of feelings and reality, escape into dreams or eccentric behaviour and general ungroundedness. Make some of the changes you have dreamed of.
- If you are contemplating self-employment there is much to recommend this. Ensure that you do not become out of touch with 'ordinary' ways of thinking and being, for you will need other people at some stage.

6 Healthy, wealthy
– and wise?

Too nice for a statesman, too proud for a wit:
For a patriot, too cool; for a drudge disobedient;
And too fond of the right to pursue the expedient.

Oliver Goldsmith

■ HEALTH

Aquarian habits may be unpredictable, and many Aquarians have things to preoccupy them other than the following of a healthy lifestyle. Often you expect your body to serve your mind tirelessly, and you are amazed and thwarted when it lets you down. This is a stoical sign, apt to ignore its own needs, expecting to be able to transcend ailments, dietary requirements and the need for recreation and exercise. Aquarians tend to push themselves to the limit serving the needs of others. Often you are too stubborn to admit you are worn out and insist on going on until you drop. This can be a strain on the system.

Being open to new ideas, Aquarians are not infrequently found at the vanguard of diet crazes and may be ready to accept all manner of explanations and theories except common sense - get to bed early, eat sensibly and have some fun. Aquarians may be erratic and impatient, going from vegetarianism to veganism to macrobiotics, detox diet, high fibre, low fat and then throw their hands in the air and reach for a chocolate bar and a tin of spaghetti, because nothing has worked and they can't be bothered. Lots of Aquarians have an especial love for animals, and so they may well choose not to eat meat, which is fine, but you must pay extra attention to content if your diet is to be nutritious. For instance, iron absorption, which is important in the transfer of oxygen in the blood, may be a problem. Iron is not always readily absorbed from sources that are high in it such as eggs and spinach, and it is worth bearing in mind that vitamin C increases iron absorption when eaten with iron-rich foods.

Aquarians may nurture the notion that somehow, somewhere, there exists the perfect way of eating, but they may not have the patience to find out what is really best for them. Other Aquarians, especially males, give little thought to what passes their lips as long as it satisfies hunger. Some may be quite cranky, with phobias about germs, while others are faddy in the extreme. This is all connected with the Aquarian wish for purity in most spheres.

Aquarian repression of feelings, that we have noted time and time again, may also be a drain on health, because these feelings surface as physical symptoms, or as weird allergies that defy diagnosis. On the plus side, Aquarians are usually open to exploring links between their minds and their bodies, and having identified a problem will work earnestly to eradicate it. Usually you far prefer to track down the cause of a headache or stomach problem than simply to take a pill, aware that tension or emotional upset has bought about the problem.

Shins and circulation

Aquarius is said to rule the shins and ankles, and because of this there may be aches and pains in the lower part of the legs. Too much effort put into metaphorical 'standing tall' often seems to undermine the parts of the body that have to work at doing this in a literal fashion. Aquarians are often no stranger to bad backs and aching legs. In addition, Aquarians may have 'cold spots' on the body, and may be subject to poor circulation and hardening of the arteries. These conditions may correlate with an idealistic disposition that is also rather inflexible.

To counteract these tendencies, the cure-all of regular walks can certainly be of help, because it offers a feeling of freedom, plenty of fresh air and stimulation for the cardiovascular system. However, it is most important for you to learn to be gentle with yourself and to treat yourself with love and caring, neither to push yourself too hard, nor to be too stoical. Sometimes you become ill because that is the only way your body can get the nurture it needs, and the only way – albeit obliquely – that you can ask for help. Massage will relax and warm you, and the physical contact is especially beneficial to your detached disposition.

■ MONEY

This sign is generally fairly 'good' with money, for three reasons. You are rarely extravagant or self-indulgent, and so the money tends to stay put – in the bank. In addition, money is of little importance to you for its own sake, and because of this it somehow accumulates unnoticed, while you do something that just happens to earn it. Also you hate to be out of control, in debt or financially beholden, and because of this you tend to keep a close hold on the purse strings.

Occasionally, Aquarians can be just a little mean. This is not intentional, but this sign often does not understand the needs of others to receive little presents and tokens of love, or attention lavished on them in the shape of a luxurious meal or lavish entertainment. Again, that need for control may mean that Aquarians have short arms and deep pockets. To many of us, money is a dirty word. Western society is focussed upon the rapacious gaining of wealth and profit, and yet most of us are a little mealy-mouthed about asking for money when it is owed to us or being seen as miserly (even when we have thousands stashed away) or out to make a 'fast buck'. Aquarius is no exception, and while you may expect to be paid what you are worth when doing a job of work, to appear to be overly concerned with money would be beneath the Water Bearer. So, in some respects, this sign may not deal well with 'filthy lucre' because you do not wish to face up to your ordinary, human need for it and the touch of acquisitiveness that is within all of us. So any Aquarian 'meanness' is likely to be quite unconscious. You may remind yourself that money is energy – no more, no less – and it needs to be channelled wisely, and well.

■ WISDOM

It is important for Aquarius to acquire wisdom in life and most Aquarians have thought long and deeply about their opinions and philosophies. Generally, your views are considered and well worth listening to, because you are capable of true detachment. Aquarians come to conclusions that are quite uninfluenced by conventional viewpoints, and so you can be quite startlingly illuminating. You are capable of taking many different factors and viewpoints into account and you often have intelligent things to say about the human race as a whole. The only drawback may be that you do not always see what is under your nose and are too apt to disregard the emotional needs of yourself and others as part of the equation. An Aquarian who also has respect for practical realities and true feelings is the wisest. You should try to avoid the impulse to find an answer for everything, for sometimes the acceptance that there is no answer is the wisest course of all.

■ PRACTICE AND CHANGE ■

Health

● If you are to behave in the way you wish, to come up to your own expectations and to discharge your obligations – or if you wish simply to maintain yourself at the peak of resourcefulness and inventiveness, then you know you must look after yourself. It is only logical.

● Although your mind may be well into the twenty-first century, your body has evolved little – if at all – since the time of our cave-dwelling ancestors. Do not inflict fads, fancies or neglect on a Palaeolithic alimentary tract.

● Pamper yourself. It is good practice for all of us to spend at least half an hour a day doing something purely for sheer, utter enjoyment. Do you do that?

● You can lie to your mind, but not your body. Look to your body for the truth about your emotions and your needs. Is it telling you something?

● Do not let your pride and 'self-sufficiency' get in the way of following the well-known guidelines about cardiovascular health. Remember '*A healthy mind in a healthy body*'.

Wealth

● Money is energy – use it as such and do not be afraid to admit that you like having, acquiring and spending money. There isn't anything wrong with that.

● Things that may not mean much to you may mean a great deal to loved ones. Aquarian women, usually more aware of their own needs than the men, may appreciate this, but Aquarian males may miss out. Make sure that you are generous with those you love.

7 Style and leisure

*If this is coffee, I want tea;
but if this is tea, then I wish for coffee*

Punch

■ YOUR LEISURE

Aquarians often love the open air – like the other Air signs, you literally need your Element for some of the time. However, Aquarians are not necessarily sporty. Some are not very well co-ordinated, physically, and this is not a competitive sign, at least not overtly. It is deeply satisfying to some Aquarians to be able to interact with their environment, for in so doing they are expressing respect for the freedom and beauty of the natural world and also bringing their minds to bear upon organising it.

Most Aquarians come into their own in some role in clubs and/or societies. This suits your need for company but also your wish to remain an impartial friend to all. You need constant mental stimulation and contact with other minds, without giving yourself too exclusively. All manner of subjects could appeal, from 'New Age' to scientific or eccentric. Many Aquarians, of course, thoroughly enjoy going out for a drink with everyone else!

Spare time is often as important to Aquarius as work, and you may feel it is almost a 'duty' to go from place to place, earnestly making contacts. Investigation of all types appeals and you can be an amateur psychologist. You like to see new plays, listen to professional storytellers and sample ethnic performances of dance, music and theatre. You can be a 'culture-vulture' always knowing about the most interesting up-and-coming event – rarely the latest mainstream blockbuster film or band, but more 'fringe' events. Life is a journey to 'find the self' and for Aquarius this is as readily, if not more so, found away from work as at work. On the other hand, if work is interesting and vocational it can absorb Aquarius utterly, to the point of obsession. In addition, there are the more dutiful 'Saturnian' Aquarians who put business before pleasure.

Aquarius hates to be bored. Sometimes you are hard to please and contrary. You are attracted to the unusual, of all kinds. Often you find greatest stimulation reading, or just thinking.

Holidays

These should not be run of the mill; avoid package tours like the plague. Many Aquarians like camping, because of the independence so afforded, and may even hitch-hike across a continent, sampling native life at close quarters, sleeping on the floor in mud hut and tepee, and loving every minute. Others like to go on holidays where retreat, meditation or study are part of the package. More 'ordinary' Aquarians should still not tie themselves to any holiday where they will be regimented. There should be plenty of opportunity to chat to the natives, and Aquarians may try to speak in the local language, even if this amounts to only several syllables. Aquarians often have a way of getting themselves accepted by people of other nationalities and can even be taken deeply into their confidence or initiated into wisdom teachings. More usually, Aquarians like to sample local history and art. Of course, plenty of Aquarians opt for a fortnight of sea, sand and sun on the Costa Mucho – but that requirement of freedom, variety and exploration still needs to be borne in mind.

■ YOUR STYLE

Aquarians, especially the males, may assert that they couldn't care less what things look like and are interested only in what is serviceable and leaves them free to pursue whatever is most important at the time. Some make an artform of scruffiness; this is a form of rebellion and not as casual as it may appear. Others are attracted to anything unusual or ethnic and may delight in wearing the shoes they bought in Ecuador, the shirt they bought in a Hong Kong market and a relic of 1960s 'Flower-power' in a psychedelic kipper tie – all at once. More usually, clothes are less extreme in character, but Aquarians go for comfort and a flavour of the unusual. Rarely are you happy in formal attire and if you are forced to wear suits you will usually manage to dress them down. Aquarian women may have real pizzazz, with a flair for creating an individual and flattering look from the contents of a rag-bag.

Around the house Aquarius like to have all the mod-cons for you have better things to do than housework. Occasionally, a minimalist taste prevails, with barely a cupboard door-knob disturbing the sleek, futuristic perfection. Others prefer a rustic ambience, with logs piled in the porch and furniture individually made, in solid wood. Sometimes the effect can be exotic and eclectic, with a totem pole in the hall, a mini cairn of stones on the window sill (picked up on memorable walks), Gilbert Williams' prints fighting for space with African carvings on the walls, and something hanging over the mantlepiece that looks like the insides of a radio. Again, this is by no means always so extreme, but a flavour of the unusual can often be detected. Aquarius likes comfortable furniture that requires little maintenance and as much space as possible for books, magazines and special artefacts. Everything should be organised so as to present the minimum of bother, leaving Aquarius with time to think, or pursue interests. State-of-the-art computer or hi-fi equipment may be in evidence.

When selecting purchases for yourself or your home think modern, unusual, futuristic, ethnic, comfortable, useful, interesting, labour saving, aura of the mystical, inventive. Some Aquarians like to have 'New Age' artefacts like crystals and dream-catchers, while others may feel they're 'naff'. Aquarian surroundings should either present no problems or challenges, leaving Aquarius free, or be an expression of individualistic tastes. Provincial and bourgeois this sign is not.

■ PRACTICE AND CHANGE ■

- Free time should involve fresh air and the opportunity to adventure in mind and/or body.

- Groups are important to Aquarius, because they offer mental stimulation and variety. If you are not involved in a group or society that supports your interests, why not give it a try?

- Aquarian spare time is intensely important – in a sense, it isn't 'spare' but devoted to that essential business of self-discovery. Ensure that you use yours well.

- Holidays should be unusual and offer new stimulation and independence. You should have relaxed and also learnt something and expanded yourself.

- Try not to be critical, erratic and contrary when in situations where you are supposed to be finding pleasure and entertainment.

- Get rid of anything boring or constricting from your wardrobe; if it isn't expressing you, then it isn't leaving you free to be yourself.

- Your home space needs to be original but also comfortable. Get rid of anything that requires a lot of maintenance, restricts space or movement, or is just plain boring.

- Give yourself time to meditate or reflect, in your home, and work out what would make it more homely and expressive of you.

Appendix 1

■ AQUARIUS COMBINED WITH MOON SIGN

Our 'birth sign' or 'star sign' refers to the sign of the zodiac occupied by the Sun when we were born. This is also called our 'Sun sign' and this book is concerned with Aquarius as a Sun sign. However, as we saw in the Introduction, a horoscope means much more than the position of the Sun alone. All the other planets have to be taken into consideration by an astrologer. Of great importance is the position of the Moon.

The Moon completes a tour of the zodiac in about twenty-eight days, changing sign every two days or so. The Moon relates to our instincts, responses, reactions, habits, comfort zone and 'where we live' emotionally – and sometimes physically. It is very important in respect of our intuitional abilities and our capacity to feel part of our environment, but because what the Moon rules is usually non-verbal and non-rational, it has been neglected. This has meant that our lives have become lop-sided. Learning to be friends with our instincts can lead to greater well-being and wholeness.

Consult the table on page 81 to find which sign the Moon was in, at the time of your birth. This, combined with your Sun sign is a valuable clue to deeper understanding.

Find your Moon number

Look up your month and day of birth. Then read across to find your personal Moon number. Now go to Chart 2, below.

January		February		March		April		May		June	
1,2	1	1,2	3	1,2	3	1,2	5	1,2	6	1,2	8
3,4	2	3,4	4	3,4	4	3,4	6	3,4	7	3,4	9
5,6	3	5,6	5	5,6	5	5,6	7	5,6	8	5,6,7	10
7,8	4	7,8	6	7,8	6	7,8	8	7,8	9	8,9	11
9,10	5	9,10,11	7	9,10	7	9,10,11	9	9,10	10	10,11,12	12
11,12	6	12,13	8	11,12	8	12,13	10	11,12,13	11	13,14	1
13,14	7	14,15	9	13,14	9	14,15,16	11	14,15,16	12	15,16,17	2
15,16,17	8	16,17,18	10	15,16,17	10	17,18	12	17,18	1	18,19	3
18,19	9	19,20	11	18,19	11	19,20,21	1	19,20	2	20,21	4
20,21	10	21,22,23	12	20,21,22	12	22,23	2	21,22,23	3	22,23	5
22,23,24	11	24,25	1	23,24,25	1	24,25	3	24,25	4	24,25	6
25,26	12	26,27,28	2	26,27	2	26,27,28	4	26,27	5	26,27	7
27,28,29	1	29	3	28,29	3	29,30	5	28,29	6	28,29,30	8
30,31	2			30,31	4			30,31	7		

July		August		September		October		November		December	
1,2	9	1	10	1,2	12	1,2	1	1,2,3	3	1,2	4
3,4	10	2,3	11	3,4	1	3,4	2	4,5	4	3,4	5
5,6,7	11	4,5,6	12	5,6,7	2	5,6	3	6,7	5	5,6	6
8,9	12	7,8	1	8,9	3	7,8,9	4	8,9	6	7,8,9	7
10,11,12	1	9,10	2	10,11	4	10,11	5	10,11	7	10,11	8
13,14	2	11,12,13	3	12,13	5	12,13	6	12,13	8	12,13	9
15,16	3	14,15	4	14,15	6	14,15	7	14,15	9	14,15	10
17,18	4	16,17	5	16,17	7	16,17	8	16,17,18	10	16,17	11
19,20	5	18,19	6	18,19	8	18,19	9	19,20	11	18,19,20	12
21,22,23	6	20,21	7	20,21,22	9	20,21	10	21,22,23	12	21,22	1
24,25	7	22,23	8	23,24	10	22,23,24	11	24,25	1	23,24,25	2
26,27	8	24,25	9	25,26,27	11	25,26	12	26,27,28	2	26,27	3
28,29	9	26,27,28	10	28,29	12	27,28,29	1	29,30	3	28,29	4
30,31	10	29,30	11	30	1	30,31	2			30,31	5
		31	12								

Find your Moon sign

Find your year of birth. Then read across to the column of your Moon number. Where they intersect shows your Moon sign.

Birth year	Moon number 1	2	3	4	5	6	7	8	9	10	11	12
1900 1919 1938 1957 1976	Cap	Aqu	Pis	Ari	Tau	Gem	Can	Leo	Vir	Lib	Sco	Sag
1901 1920 1939 1958 1977	Tau	Gem	Can	Leo	Vir	Lib	Sco	Sag	Cap	Aqu	Pis	Ari
1902 1921 1940 1959 1978	Lib	Sco	Sag	Cap	Aqu	Pis	Ari	Tau	Gem	Can	Leo	Vir
1903 1922 1941 1960 1979	Aqu	Pis	Ari	Tau	Gem	Can	Leo	Vir	Lib	Sco	Sag	Cap
1904 1923 1942 1961 1980	Gem	Can	Leo	Vir	Lib	Sco	Sag	Cap	Aqu	Pis	Ari	Tau
1905 1924 1943 1962 1981	Sco	Sag	Cap	Aqu	Pis	Ari	Tau	Gem	Can	Leo	Vir	Lib
1906 1925 1944 1963 1982	Pis	Ari	Tau	Gem	Can	Leo	Vir	Lib	Sco	Sag	Cap	Aqu
1907 1926 1945 1964 1983	Leo	Vir	Lib	Sco	Sag	Cap	Aqu	Pis	Ari	Tau	Gem	Can
1908 1927 1946 1965 1984	Sag	Cap	Aqu	Pis	Ari	Tau	Gem	Can	Leo	Vir	Lib	Sco
1909 1928 1947 1966 1985	Ari	Tau	Gem	Can	Leo	Vir	Lib	Sco	Sag	Cap	Aqu	Pis
1910 1929 1948 1967 1986	Vir	Lib	Sco	Sag	Cap	Aqu	Pis	Ari	Tau	Gem	Can	Leo
1911 1930 1949 1968 1987	Cap	Aqu	Pis	Ari	Tau	Gem	Can	Leo	Vir	Lib	Sco	Sag
1912 1931 1950 1969 1988	Gem	Can	Leo	Vir	Lib	Sco	Sag	Cap	Aqu	Pis	Ari	Tau
1913 1932 1951 1970 1989	Lib	Sco	Sag	Cap	Aqu	Pis	Ari	Tau	Gem	Can	Leo	Vir
1914 1933 1952 1971 1990	Pis	Ari	Tau	Gem	Can	Leo	Vir	Lib	Sco	Sag	Cap	Aqu
1915 1934 1953 1972 1991	Can	Leo	Vir	Lib	Sco	Sag	Cap	Aqu	Pis	Ari	Tau	Gem
1916 1935 1954 1973 1992	Sco	Sag	Cap	Aqu	Pis	Ari	Tau	Gem	Can	Leo	Vir	Lib
1917 1936 1955 1974 1993	Ari	Tau	Gem	Can	Leo	Vir	Lib	Sco	Sag	Cap	Aqu	Pis
1918 1937 1956 1975 1994	Leo	Vir	Lib	Sco	Sag	Cap	Aqu	Pis	Ari	Tau	Gem	Can

Ari Tau Gem Can Leo Vir Lib Sco Sag Cap Aqu Pis

Aquarius Sun / Aquarius Moon

You are a true individual. You think for yourself and may have some very avant-garde ideas – possibly you are resourceful about putting these into practice. An abstract and intuitive thinker for the most part, you like to interact with a wide variety of people and it may well be important to you to feel you contribute something to society at large. You are a radical, able to approach almost any subject with a clear and unbiased attitude and quite prepared to stampede sacred cows. Often it seems amazing to you that other people cannot see what is as plain as the noses on their faces. What you may be missing is the feeling dimension of experience. People are more likely to give you a fair hearing if you take into account their tender spots. Emotions are important; they bind society. In your search for freedom are you giving yourself emotional freedom, or are you determined not to feel too much, get too close or needy, or feel undesirable things? In your circle of friends, make sure you include those who can accept your inner sensitivity and also help you to accept it.

Aquarius Sun / Pisces Moon

You are both an idealist and a dreamer. Possibly you cannot see why we can't have Utopia – now! You like to feel you have empathy with others and that you can help them. In fact, you can lose yourself in other people's needs, while being too noble to acknowledge your own. It is hard for you to accept some aspects of reality, for you have a divine discontent. Make sure you have a theatre in life where you can translate some of your dreams into reality – but brace yourself for the fact that they may fall far short of what you envisage. This is better than nothing. Do allow yourself to experience the pain, vulnerability and neediness within you, for we all have this and you can't effectively talk yourself out of it. If you are honest with yourself about your feelings then you are more likely to be a channel for the creative and inspired.

Aquarius Sun / Aries Moon

You have lots of dreams and schemes and you are also dynamic – you like to see action. You can accomplish a great deal, for your plans are powered by inner passion and conviction. Sometimes your strong desire may make you feel a little uncomfortable, and you may tell yourself you can do without the satisfaction of your own needs. You are an independent person and it may seem, sometimes, that while you are needing to get close, at the same time you are pulling away. You can be impulsive. Although you can accomplish a great deal, you may not be well grounded in your physical body, and the abstract may seem almost as tangible as the concrete. You may be in search of excitement, stimulation and new ideas, wishing to push back the boundaries of experience, but you may rarely feel deeply satisfied. Try to achieve a sense of having both feet on the ground so you can be sure of what you really need. In the long run, momentary satisfaction will not do – give yourself time to find what is really important to you, rather than what you would like to be important, or what seems thrilling at the time.

Aquarius Sun / Taurus Moon

Just a little stubborn, are you, at times? You do not like to let go of things, people or ideas, but you are also an idealist. This could sometimes result in your being dogmatic about what you believe to be a principle which is, in fact, something that is serving your own ends. You need to be honest with yourself about your motives and acknowledge that there is conflict within you – there is no harm in that. You need security, reassurance and sensual gratification; you also need to have ideals for which to aim. Possibly you adopt a rigid self-sufficiency which denies your deeper requirements. Give yourself permission to gratify your essential needs and enjoy yourself – and give others the freedom to do the same. Although this isn't an easy combination, it is potentially a most creative and dynamic one, and you can give a solid basis to your theories and visions: that can be the most satisfying of all.

Aquarius Sun/Gemini Moon

You are probably a sociable and friendly person with an enquiring and original mind. Possibly you think quickly, seeing things from all angles and coming up with some original ideas. You like to know what is going on, and where, and you have informed opinions on many subjects – probably you are 'clever'. Resourceful, versatile and inventive, you can turn your mind to many matters – what you may not wish to acknowledge are your emotions, and you may rationalise these. You may escape from them into ceaseless chatter or to restlessly moving from one diversion to another, which conveniently prevents you from getting too close to anyone. Turn your mind to some self-examination so that you can build a life that is emotionally nurturing as well as mentally stimulating. You can make the best of your many abilities if you do not spread yourself too thinly, and your excellent mental powers will serve you better if you are not so highly strung you cannot settle. In some ways things may seem to run smoothly for you, but don't let that prevent you from trying to improve.

Aquarius Sun / Cancer Moon

You are a caring person and may try to look after a wide variety of people and things – friends, family, even the environment. Your idealism is backed up by some real sympathy and you may try to do everything for everybody, putting yourself last. What may be really difficult for you is to look after yourself, and yet there is a part of you that cries out to be looked after. This may surface as just a touch of the 'martyr' in you at times, or it may mean that you gratify yourself indirectly, perhaps by eating too much or similar, while denying what you really want. Try to care for yourself first, not last. This may appear selfish, and not even terribly gratifying, because it is so much nicer if other people sense what you need and provide it – but life isn't like that! However, if your own requirements are met you will be a healthier and more stable individual and so much more able to give to others what you are so good at giving – your care.

Aquarius Sun / Leo Moon

Here we have an internal dilemma, for on the one hand you like to appear detached, independent and a little aloof (while being generally friendly) but on the other you have a deep need to be the centre of attention. Sometimes you may embarrass yourself by your efforts to claim the limelight. At others you may be frustrated at not being noticed. You can either express this by being bossy and a bit cranky and overbearing, or you can work to resolve this, so your warm and playful heart can empower your idealism and originality. You can work for a healthy objectivity – as opposed to detachment – and strive to balance your inner nature. Thus, while you need to bask in attention and to be spontaneous, you also need to be detached and objective. These are not mutually incompatible as

long as you are conscious of what is happening and do not blow hot
and cold. Learn to provide honestly, for your own emotions; don't
hope for this to come from an audience all the time, but do expect
legitimate reward for your creativity. You can be dynamic and
inspired. Take note of your dreams, for these may be significant.

Aquarius Sun / Virgo Moon

You have an analytical approach, expecting perfection in most
things and wanting to do everything to the best of your ability. You
may give yourself little space to fail, being self-critical – and you may
be critical of other people, too. You like to be helpful, useful and
organised. Personal integrity is one of your priorities. You are wonderfully thorough and efficient, but you also like to keep the
purpose and the overview in sight, seeing both the wood and the
trees: this is highly desirable and can mean you achieve a great deal,
but it can be stressful. It is probably hard for you to be spontaneous,
for you are prone to worry about doing the right thing and keeping
busy. You have an idealistic personality as well as an eye for detail,
so always be prepared to review your priorities with a clear and
unbiased eye. Value the sheer humanity in yourself and others, and
do not be so hard on yourself – there is more to life than 'shoulds'
and 'oughts', so let the rebel out.

Aquarius Sun / Libra Moon

Generally, you are a high-minded soul, extremely idealistic about the
human spirit and liking to see the best in everyone. In fact, you sometimes refuse to see emotional murk, assuming everyone is good and
true. Although there is nobility in this, there is also some self-decep-
tion. You are a person who needs company and hates conflict, and so

it can be easier to pretend we are all angels. However, until you do face this aspect of humanity – and yourself – your relationships are unlikely to achieve depth and the true harmony you crave. There is something in you of both the diplomat and the philosopher and you can be pleasant to be around. You have a strong sense of the beautiful. Seek out peace and loveliness, by all means, but remember that true beauty is not skin deep. It may sometimes be necessary to endure discord to achieve real honesty and contact with another person.

Aquarius Sun/Scorpio Moon

This is a dynamic and potentially explosive combination that will need scorching self-honesty to make the best of yourself. On the one hand you have the Aquarian attributes of detachment, objectivity and impartiality, while on the other you have the powerful passions of your Scorpionic core. The danger is that you may deny your deepest needs, regarding them as 'unworthy', translating them perhaps into sexuality and subtle control of others, whom you then see as demanding, jealous and over-emotional – but this is a situation that you are probably causing yourself, at least in part. If you can be aware of this you have the potential to draw upon reserves of power and knowledge of human experience that will add considerable force to all you undertake, giving you depth as well as idealism and vitalising your ideas with an inner passion. Remember it's okay to feel *anything* – it's what you do with it that counts.

Aquarius Sun/Sagittarius Moon

For the most part you are cheerful, philosophical and optimistic. Freedom is important to you, conceptually and physically, and you are probably an explorer – of ideas, if nothing else. You have the tendency to concentrate on the future and possibilities rather than what is here and now: you may be a sociable person or one who is 'away with the fairies' at times. You possess a measure of internal peace, but when difficulties come knocking you may distance yourself from them by joking, escapism and restlessness. You do need an inner, spiritual belief to help you come to terms with, rather than avoid your feelings. Be generous with yourself as well as others and be emotionally honest as well as straight in other respects. Cultivate an inner freedom which means you can 'do willingly that which must be done' rather than avoiding issues.

Aquarius Sun / Capricorn Moon

At times you may be a little gloomy and may prefer your own company, feeling more comfortable with detachment. You may have a stern internal 'parent voice' that speaks of duty, self-sufficiency and moral conduct. You have the gift both of originality and inventiveness, and the ability to create practical structures for your ideas – be careful to get these qualities in balance, so they support each other, rather than allowing negativity and emphasis upon difficulties to distract you from your overall purpose. Concentrate on developing your own standards that come from an unbiased approach that is fair to *you* and your needs. Cultivate also the strength to be vulnerable – to say 'I need' and 'I feel', and to do something about this. You can be truly independent – and at the same time achieve meaningful closeness with others – only when you have learnt to take proper care of yourself as opposed to saying 'I can do without'.

Appendix 2

ZODIACAL COMPATIBILITY

To assess fully the compatibility of two people the astrologer needs to have the entire chart of each individual, and while Sun-sign factors will be noticeable, there is a legion of other important points to be taken into account. Venus and Mercury are always very close to the Sun, and while these are often in the Sun sign, so intensifying its effect, they may also fall in one of the signs lying on either side of your Sun sign. So, as an Aquarius you may have Venus and/or Mercury in Capricorn or Pisces, and this will increase your empathy with these signs. In addition the Moon and all the other planets including the Ascendant and Midheaven need to be taken into account. So if you have always been drawn to Cancerian people, maybe you have Moon or Ascendant in Cancer.

In order to give a vivid character sketch things have to be stated graphically. You should look for the dynamics at work rather than be too literal about interpretation – for instance, you may find you do not have much difficulty with Taureans, but you may be aware of a great difference in approach to life. It is up to the two of you whether a relationship works for it can if you are both committed. Part of that is using the awareness you have to help, not necessarily as a reason for abandoning the relationship. There are always points of compatibility, and we are here to learn from each other.

On a scale of 1 (worst) to 4 (best), here is a table to assess instantly the superficial compatibility rating between Aquarius and companions:

Aquarius 3	Leo 1
Pisces 2	Virgo 3
Aries 2	Libra 4
Taurus 1	Scorpio 2
Gemini 4	Sagittarius 4
Cancer 1	Capricorn 1

■ AQUARIUS COMPATIBILITIES

Aquarius with Aquarius

It's a little miracle that two such detached and preoccupied souls ever manage to touch base together – but it does happen! As you are both so high-minded and noble, who gets to carry the coal sack of emotional needs, childishness and occasional 'nastiness' that is the legacy of all human flesh? You may each be conscious of the other's warts, while seeing yourself as the long-suffering one. Aquarians are truthful and humane, but true emotional honesty is an immense task for them. Nonetheless, you both mean well.

As lovers   Unless both of you have planets in Water and Fire signs, you are not prone to passion. However, you should understand each other's needs very well. Mr Aquarius is delighted to have found such an impartial and original lady, and Ms Aquarius enjoys the company of this free spirit. It is possible that the relationship could lack emotional depth and you may blame each other for this. It is so important to be honest with yourselves and each other about how you feel, and to cultivate true and deep friendship – for in the end that may be the most important aspect of your relationship.

As friends   Naturally you are likely to have much in common and may enjoy socialising together, studying, investigating, theorising and setting the world to rights. On the other hand, you might fight perpetually, each believing he or she is always right.

As business partners This could work well, especially if one of you is the innovative type of Aquarius and the other the more cautious. However, there is, again, the possible problem of 'who's right?'

Aquarius with Pisces

There is much to attract the two of you, for you are both visionary, idealistic and dreamy in your different ways. Being intensely humanitarian, compassionate and aware of other dimensions, it may seem that life has opened a golden door through which you can pass and live happily ever after. Not so fast! Deep within, the dynamics of these two signs are vastly different, for Pisces resonates to feeling, while Aquarius elevates thought. The danger is that Pisces may prove too elusive, inconsistent and emotional for Aquarius, while Pisces can be cut to the quick by Aquarian insensitivity and erratic response.

As lovers Passions may run high at first. Pisces displays all the richness of feeling for which Aquarius secretly yearns, while the Fish is electrified by the Water Bearer, and life may seem quite magical. Ms Aquarius warms to this sensitive, generous character, while Mr Aquarius is entranced by mysterious Pisces. Slowly, realisation may dawn that you are coming from different corners of the galaxy. Everything now depends on whether Aquarius can find at least a respect for emotional fluidity and expression – and find emotional honesty within – and whether Pisces can acquire detachment and a value for Aquarian impartiality. You two have much to offer each other or you can make a misery of each other's lives. When you're good together, you're very, very good, and when you're bad – you're horrid! Work at it.

As friends   Again there is much that is shared on the idealistic front. However, Aquarius probably does not understand Piscean need for empathy, and may try to tell Pisces what to do – exit Pisces. A little distance between you can help, but not too much.

As business partners   With a cautious Aquarian this could work.

Aquarius with Aries

Aquarius may patronise Aries a little, as an *enfant terrible* and may admire the Arien flare and independence. This can be quite an electric partnership. Aries' habit of acting first and thinking later may send Aquarius into a network of analysing and rationalising, which Aries will usually ignore, until Aquarius informs Aries what to think, and what the Ram should do in the future. Fireworks! However, this relationship is often one of mutual respect.

As lovers   Whacky and inventive at first, although both may tire of the relationship, and Aquarius is likely to prove a little too cool for Aries in the long run, while Aries may come on as demanding. Mr Aquarius is riveted by the enterprise and *élan* of Ms Aries, while Ms Aquarius feels that this is a stimulating man to be with. Each of these two may embark on extra-marital affairs, and it is possible that an 'open marriage' could exist. Aries is likely to cope with Aquarian detachment by looking for pastures new, but may feel rejected and puzzled. Aquarius, too, can feel hurt and Aries may make the Water Bearer jealous, although Aquarius would probably never admit to it! To get the best of this relationship Aries needs to verbalise without being biting, and Aquarius needs to listen.

As friends   A stimulating friendship, with lots of interchange and debate. You will both be looking for a good time and can find it together. Never a dull moment, always something new and exciting to do.

As business partners   Both of you are innovative and adventurous, but there could be problems over money with the more 'Uranian' type of Aquarian. Aquarius is good at weighing up Aries' schemes and may spot subtleties that the Ram has missed.

Aquarius with Taurus

These signs share little, apart from stubbornness! – and yet they are often strongly attracted. There is something about the solid sensuality of Taurus that Aquarius cannot define or analyse, but that doesn't prevent Aquarius trying.

As lovers   Sex may be good, although the more-ishness of Taurus may be too much for Aquarius to handle, and the Water Bearer may head for the free air like a guided missile. Taurus can be driven to extremes of jealousy and outrage by Aquarius, and the latter may make accusations about being 'tied down' – but the truth is that neither likes change much and they may struggle on together for years. There is something about the solidity of the Bull that can earth Aquarian thunderbolts, and each may agree to differ and live in reasonable contentment. Ms Aquarius finds this man's self-assurance and basic sensuality rather magnetic, as long as he isn't too demanding, while Mr Aquarius may ponder long and deeply what makes Ms Taurus so sexy, following up his theories with experimentation. Each does provide what the other needs, and the trick is to appreciate this fact.

As friends   Aquarius enjoys debate, but Taurus calls it an 'argument'. Aquarius may be scornful at this, or may feel unutterably frustrated. Both of you are 'always right' and it may be possible to maintain a comfortable distance with this conviction in place! Taurus sometimes feels – almost reluctantly – interested in unusual subjects encouraged by Aquarius, while Taurus injects common sense, so there are aspects to offer each other.

As business partners   Possibly good; Taurus with money, Aquarius with ideas.

Aquarius with Gemini

In many ways these two Air signs are made for each other. Both of you have quick and active minds and an avid interest in life – enjoy exploring it together.

As lovers   There may be lots of talk and flirting but not much action. Neither of you is especially passionate (unless there are significant planets in Earth or Fire) and although onlookers may think that sex is all you think about, 'think' is the operative word. To both of you the mind is the most erogenous zone. Stylish and inventive erotica may fascinate you both, and you may feel that sex is great for you. Ms Aquarius loves this man's quick wit and gift for repartee, while Mr Aquarius is hooked by Ms Gemini, whose feminine appearance and lively mind never bore him – and that's saying something! Emotional depth may be lacking, unless there are planets in Water signs. Of greatest importance to each is the friendship content of the relationship, which is likely to prove the binding factor. Both logical, there will rarely be arguments about where to put the biscuit tin.

As friends   Although you may both describe yourselves as 'emotional' your emotions are rarely what you think they are, thus friendship can be the most comfortable dimension. There will be lots to explore, to think about and to discuss and understanding between you can be excellent.

As business partners   Gemini is often a salesperson, great at interaction with the public. Aquarius may be 'steadier' until a sudden electric impulse lights up the screen. Your enterprise could be really zippy, and then hit an unseen rock, so some solid 'Earthy' influence might help. However, you both bounce back!

Aquarius with Cancer

Air and Water signs are often attracted, and thereby hangs an all-too-frequent tale of frustration, pain and perplexity. Aquarius longs for the emotional depth of Cancer, while Cancer needs the detachment and analytical capability of Aquarius. But do they realise this? Only rarely. Aquarius may find Cancer suffocating and may write the Crab off as insecure and demanding – and yet the Water Bearer can't resist coming back to analyse, wonder, and, if the truth be told, get cared for. Cancer eternally hopes that Aquarius will one day manage to respond from the heart and show neediness. Meanwhile moods stretch like swamps, and the unpredictable falls like flour bags from the door, making this relationship an obstacle course. Something powerful brought you together – stick with it.

As lovers   Sexually this can be great, especially at first. Ms Aquarius appreciates the sensitivity of Mr Cancer – macho-men may bore her – while Mr Aquarius is drawn to the seductive depths of Cancer, telling himself she's 'interesting'. Once committed, Aquarius often does prove loyal, but the Crab will hardly be comforted by the cold performance of duty. Aquarius will perform some amazing mental contortions in order to evade true feelings, and if Cancer is secure enough in emotional telepathy to understand this, the relationship can work. Aquarius needs to work at emotional honesty and the Crab at a little detachment – it's what you both secretly want, and you are programmed to teach it to each other.

As friends   Aquarius can widen Cancer's perspectives while Cancer can give Aquarius something to think about. Minus sex you may not be drawn together.

As business partners   Aquarius may make Cancer nervous. However, not a bad mix if you have separate areas – Aquarian ideas, with Cancer to handle clients and budget.

Aquarius with Leo

Here the iconoclast meets the king – and strangely, it isn't always possible to tell which is which! Aquarius may strongly resent the attention seeking of the Lion while also secretly longing for some of the limelight; Leo admires Aquarian courage to 'be different', at the same time being overtly scornful of the Water Bearer's lack of style. Both are bossy in their own way, and may see the other as a tyrant. However, you share a fun-loving streak, and Leo's need to be involved can prove a foil for Aquarian detachment.

As lovers   At first, attraction may be strong, but Leo is demanding, passionate and possessive, while Aquarius is the opposite, and there may be some battle-royals that culminate in Aquarius walking out. Both of you are terminally stubborn – lock-outs and guerilla warfare could go on for weeks, with both acting superior! However, Leo can show Aquarius ways to project individuality and turn ideals into gold, while Aquarius can give Leo a dash of objectivity. Ms Aquarius may be agog at Mr Leo's charm and charisma, while Mr Aquarius is dazzled by the 'star quality' of Leo. Remember what first attracted you – life is unlikely to be dull!

As friends   As long as you share a sense of humour your relationship can be good. Sometimes you will need to agree to differ. Shared ideals can result in a dynamic duo – remember to give other people a hearing, too. Don't let the Sun go down on your anger!

As business partners   Endless arguments are likely as you each feel quite convinced that you're right! Aquarius is good at lateral thinking while Leo knows how to make a brilliant impression. However, you may both be impatient with details, and Leo may think up some lordly excuses to leave Aquarius burning the midnight oil over the accounts. Share and share alike!

Aquarius with Virgo

Both of you have a rather mental orientation. Virgo may admire the detachment of the Water Bearer, while wishing Aquarius would be a little more solid and practical, while Aquarius likes the precise approach of the Virgo, but won't tolerate any fuss. The relationship will work better with the more 'Saturnian' Aquarian.

As lovers   You may enjoy experimentation at first, but Virgo may be too cool and emotionally reserved to light any fires for Aquarius – although on the plus side Virgoan restraint will be reassuring. Similarly, Aquarius may be too cerebral to coax out the sensual side of Virgo. Ms Aquarius appreciates this man's respect for her autonomy, while Mr Aquarius is attracted to the self-possession of Virgo. Sexual difficulties are possible, with neither party actually admitting there is anything wrong. You will enjoy talking, discussing, working out and analysing everything from esoterica to the planting out of your seedlings. This can be a lasting relationship but strong feeling may be absent unless there are planets in Fire and/or Water. However, neither of you may be bothered.

As friends   Virgo is helpful to Aquarius when it comes to the actual planting of Airy ideas in a fertile soil. Both of you are likely to be interested in diverse issues and may be eternally fascinated at the other's perspective – or left cold. Aquarius is rather progressive for Virgo, who may be uneasy to see convention scorned, and Aquarius may enjoy annoying Virgo at times.

As business partners   Providing Aquarian notions aren't too off-planet, Virgo may see the advantage of them. This partnership can work well if Aquarius has lots of ideas and plans are worked out together.

Aquarius with Libra

This can be a very good and easy partnership, for Libra is always open to reason and gives Aquarius plenty of breathing space. Both of you are idealists, although Libra may feel that Aquarius is a little brusque and tactless and that the Water Bearer's visions are a little stark. However, Aquarius can cope with talking about the relationship – which Libra loves to do – and Libra can take in the cultural scope of the Water Bearer – although Libra may wonder what it all has to do with the millennium and ancient Egyptian mythology.

As lovers Enthusiastic and varied at the start. Emotional swamp trips will be avoided by each, but by the same token bonding may be somewhat superficial. Sexuality may recede until friendship reigns, and that may suit Aquarius more than Libra, who needs a measure of intimacy, albeit genteel. Ms Aquarius finds this man's urbanity and ease of manner enticing, while Mr Aquarius can appreciate that this feminine lady is anything but an airhead. A good social life will be appreciated by both.

As friends There is likely to be some interesting interchange, and discussions may be fruitful because neither gets too emotional and may enjoy debate. Both of you are interested in learning about life and may relish the exploration together. Avant-garde Aquarian ideas may amuse Libra and appeal to Libran taste for the culturally superior. Aquarius resonates to Libran receptiveness and can lead Libra into new pastures by force of argument.

As business partners Aquarius may be impatient of Libran preoccupation with making a good impression, and may want available funds to be spent on updating technology rather than 'dressing the window'. Auspices are best with the 'Saturnian' Aquarian, who may be good at handling money – which Libra isn't! Aquarius may be abrupt at times, so Libra should handle PR.

Aquarius with Scorpio

These two can often not leave each other alone, despite enormous differences in temperament. Aquarian passions are generally sub-terranean but Scorpio may provide the earthquake to unleash them. A wise Scorpio senses all the buried emotions that Aquarius doesn't realise he or she has, and may play emotional games. However, while Scorpio is intense, there is also considerable control, and the Scorpion may play it just as cool as Aquarius. Both signs are strong, stubborn and resistant to change.

As lovers Sexually this may be a magnetic partnership. Scorpio inspires Aquarius to inventiveness and compelling response, while the Aquarian 'otherness' can be fascinating to Scorpio. Ms Aquarius is drawn to this smoky individual, while Mr Aquarius is endlessly intrigued by the smoulder and restraint of Scorpio. In the long run, Aquarius may feel caught in some invisible web, while Scorpio may be in a state of torment due to the wandering habits of Aquarius. Scorpio may go ballistic, or may simmer with repressed rage and pain. However, you each see much to admire in the other, for you are both tough characters. Aquarius secretly longs to find such depths internally, and Scorpio is intrigued by Aquarian mental processes. Hang on in there!

As friends You both have an interest in the boundaries of human experience, so although your approaches may be quite different, you may find each other interesting. You will have to agree to differ on occasion.

As business partners Scorpio can smell a rat at a hundred paces and this can be a foil for Aquarian idealism about human nature! As long as mutual respect is maintained, this partnership could be dynamic. A third party might help with PR.

Aquarius with Sagittarius

These two signs get on well together, for they share a philosophical attitude and a broad conceptual framework. Each needs to be free, and there could be some competition for who can breeze off the most and who gets left holding the baby. Life is usually fun together, and you are both adept at turning your backs on any difficulties – sometimes this means they magically go away; at others unresolved issues turn up to bite you on the posterior!

As lovers   There may be lots of sexual enthusiasm at first, but this may get diverted into other highways and byways. Aquarius may be too remote for the Fiery Sagittarian, but there is always sure to be common ground. Ms Aquarius finds this man amusing and stimulating, and he may make her laugh, which is great. Mr Aquarius feels he can relax and expand with this woman who is just as much a free spirit as he is, and has so many interesting experiences and *Lebenslust*. Being 'good mates' and co-adventurers is likely to be important to you both.

As friends   Like many Aquarian partnerships, friendship will be important to you both. You may share many philosophical, cultural and exploratory pursuits, from hillwalking to UFOlogy. Your combined circle of friends is likely to be wide, and your social life lively and spontaneous with impromptu barbecues, swapping of CDs and setting the world to rights over the garden fence. Enjoy yourselves!

As business partners   You will need to be careful here, as Aquarius may be inspired by Sagittarius and there may be no boundaries on expense and little realism. Things will be more solid with the 'Saturnian' type of Aquarian. Input from a third party with lots of Earth in the chart could help.

Aquarius with Capricorn

To outsiders this partnership looks right and tight, with both saying and doing the proper thing. Especially with the more 'Saturnian' Aquarian, we have a couple where duty predominates. Both of you may be controlled, and you are able to talk through any problems with relentless reasoning. Compromises can be found and practicality rules. Each of you has a stiff upper lip.

As lovers   Unless there are many planets in Water and Fire signs, this is likely to be a cool partnership. Ms Aquarius respects Mr Capricorn's efficient and restrained approach, and Mr Aquarius regards this woman as eminently capable, and he treasures her independence. There may be plenty of mutual appreciation, but there may also be an unspoken loneliness – and it is said that it is much more lonely to be alone in a partnership than to be truly solo. Aquarius may find Capricorn too conventional and Capricorn may be embarrassed by the more bohemian Aquarian traits. Capricorn has a yearning for physical closeness and to liberate the 'wilder' side, while Aquarius needs a companion on adventures as well as to awaken the dormant emotional response. It will be hard for these two to satisfy each other in such matters, and each will probably need to take a unilateral decision to open up. This needs a lot of self-awareness and honesty.

As friends   This could be a friendship of mutual support and loyalty, agreeing to differ on some issues, with Capricorn putting into practice Aquarian schemes, and Aquarius valuing Capricornian practicality. Friendship could endure on a cerebral level, without there being much closeness, but that may not be what you expect from each other.

As business partners   This duo may lack flair, unless Aquarian is the 'Uranian' type. However, with planning and determination success is quite possible.

Appendix 3

■ TRADITIONAL ASSOCIATIONS AND TOTEM

Each sign of the zodiac is said to have an affinity with certain colours, plants, stones and other substances. Of course, we cannot be definite about this, for not only do sources vary regarding specific correspondences – we also have the rest of the astrological chart to bear in mind. Some people also believe that the whole concept of such associations is invalid. However, there certainly do seem to be some links between the character of each of the signs and the properties of certain substances. It is up to you to experiment and to see what works for you.

Anything that traditionally links with Aquarius is liable to intensify Aquarian traits. So if you wish to be impassioned and involved, you should steer clear of the Aquarian colours and other associations listed below. Naturally you are not restricted to essential oils ruled by your sign, for in many cases treatment by other oils will be beneficial, and you should consult a reputable source for advice if you have a particular problem. However, if you want to be your Aquarian, innovative best, it may help you to surround yourself with the right stimuli, especially on a down day. Here are some suggestions:

● **Colours**   Electric blue, some shades of yellow, mustard, yellowy-brown, unusual contrasts and shades, fluorescent colours.

- **Flowers** Acacia, lavender, mimosa.
- **Metal** Uranium. Obviously this radioactive element cannot be worn or used around the home but it gives a clue to futuristic and unusual tastes.
- **Stones** Aquamarine, fossils, jet, amazonite (blue-green feldspar).

Aromatherapy

Aromatherapy uses the healing power of essential oils both to prevent ill health and to maintain good health. Specific oils can sometimes be used to treat specific ailments. Essential oils are concentrated and powerful substances, and should be treated with respect. Buy from a reputable source that it is okay (see 'Further Reading'). *Do not use any oil in pregnancy* until you have checked with a reputable source. *Do not ingest oils* – they act through the subtle medium of smell and are absorbed in massage. *Do not place undiluted on the skin.* For massage: Dilute in a carrier oil, such as sweet almond or grapeseed, two drops of oil to one teaspoon of carrier. Use in an oil burner, six to ten drops at a time, to fragrance your living area.

Essential oils
- **Benzoin** This has a sweet aroma, like vanilla. It is good for relieving nasal congestion, promotes the flow of blood and the healthy production of urine. Its warm and dry character is especially suited to Aquarius.
- **Lavender** Clear, fresh and gentle, this oil promotes peace and balance. It is good for soothing headaches, it is an analgesic and it is a tonic for the heart and for blood pressure.
- **Peppermint** Good for keeping a clear head and valuable for combatting digestive upsets. It has a cooling and stimulating action.

Your birth totem

According to the tradition of certain native North American tribes, each of the signs of the zodiac is known by a totem animal. The idea of the totem animal is useful, for animals are powerful, living symbols and they can do much to put us in touch with our own potentials. Knowing your totem animal is different from knowing your sign, for your sign is used to define and describe you – as we have been doing in this book – whereas your totem shows you a path of potential learning and growth.

The totem for Aquarius is the Otter, and you also have an affinity with Buffalo and Butterfly. You were born in the Cleansing Time. There is a difficulty here, for the North American lore is based on the seasonal cycle. Thus for those of you living in the Southern Hemisphere, it may be worth bearing in mind the totems of your opposite sign, Leo. These are Salmon, also Mouse, and possibly Hawk of the Fire clan.

Otters are playful creatures, adaptable and equally at home on land or in the water. They make loyal mates and are caring towards their young. The lesson of Otter is not to take ourselves and our concerns too seriously, to be prepared to let go and move on, 'going with the flow' and this can be helpful to Aquarians who, although they may be unpredictable, are not always as open to change as they could be. Light-hearted and fluid, Otter shows the value of spontaneity and sheer fun.

Contacting your totem

You can use visualisation techniques to make contact with the energies of your birth totem. You will need to be quiet, still and relaxed. Make sure you won't be disturbed. Have a picture of your totem before you, and perhaps burn one of the oils we have mentioned, in an oil burner, to intensify the atmosphere. When you are ready close your eyes and imagine that you are your totem animal – imagine how it feels, what it smells, sees, hears. What are its feelings, instincts and abilities? Keep this up for as long as you are comfortable, then come back to everyday awareness. Write down your experiences and eat or drink something to ground you. This can be a wonderfully refreshing and mind-clearing exercise, and you may find it inspiring. Naturally, if you feel you have other totem animals – creatures with which you feel an affinity – you are welcome to visualise these. Look out for your totems in the wild – there may be a message for you.

Further reading and resources

Astrology for Lovers, Liz Greene, Unwin, 1986. The title may be misleading, for this is a serious, yet entertaining and wickedly accurate account of the signs. A table is included to help you find your Rising Sign. This book is highly recommended.

Teach Yourself Astrology, Jeff Mayo and Christine Ramsdale, Hodder & Stoughton, 1996. A classic textbook for both beginner and practising astrologer, giving a fresh insight to birth charts through a unique system of personality interpretation.

Love Signs for Beginners, Kristyna Arcarti, Hodder & Stoughton, 1995. A practical introduction to the astrology of romantic relationships, explaining the different roles played by each of the planets and focussing particularly on the position of the Moon at the time of birth.

Star Signs for Beginners, Kristyna Arcarti, Hodder & Stoughton, 1993. An analysis of each of the star signs – a handy, quick reference.

The Moon and You for Beginners, Teresa Moorey, Hodder & Stoughton, 1996. Discover how the phase of the Moon when you were born affects your personality. This book looks at the nine lunar types – how they live, love, work and play, and provides simple tables to enable you to find out your birth phase and which type you are.

The New Compleat Astrologer, Derek and Julia Parker, Mitchell Beazley, 1984. This is a complete introduction to astrology with instructions on chart calculation and planetary tables, as well as clear and interesting descriptions of planets and signs. Including history and reviewing present-day astrology, this is an extensive work, in glossy, hardback form, with colour illustrations.

The Knot of Time: Astrology and the Female Experience, Lindsay River and Sally Gillespie. For personal growth, from a gently feminine perspective, this book has much wisdom.

The Astrology of Self-discovery, Tracy Marks, CRCS Publications, 1985. This book is especially useful for Moon signs.

The Astrologer's Handbook, Francis Sakoian and Louis Acker, Penguin, 1984. This book explains chart calculation and takes the reader through the meanings of signs and planets, with extensive interpretations of planets in signs and houses. In addition, all the major aspects between planets and angles are interpreted individually. A very useful work.

Aromatherapy for Pregnancy and Childbirth, Margaret Fawcett RGN, RM, LLSA, Element, 1993.

The Aromatherapy Handbook, Daniel Ryman, C W Daniel, 1990.

Useful addresses

The Faculty of Astrological Studies

The claim of the Faculty to provide the 'finest and most comprehensive astrological tuition in the world' is well founded. Correspondence courses of a high calibre are offered, leading to the internationally recognised diploma. Evening classes, seminars and summer schools are taught, catering for the complete beginner to the most experienced astrologer. A list of trained consultants can be supplied on request, if you wish for a chart interpretation. For further details telephone (UK code) 0171 700 3556 (24-hour answering service); or fax 0171 700 6479. Alternatively, you can write, with SAE, to: Ref. T. Moorey, FAS., BM7470, London WC1N 3XX, UK.

Educational

California Institute of Integral Studies, 765 Ashbury St, San Francisco, CA 94117. Tel: (415) 753-6100

Kepler College of Astrological Arts and Sciences, 4518 University Way, NE, Suite 213, Seattle, WA 98105. Tel: (206) 633-4907

Robin Armstrong School of Astrology, Box 5265, Station 'A', Toronto, Ontario, M5W 1N5, Canada. Tel: (416) 923-7827

Vancouver Astrology School, Astraea Astrology, Suite 412, 2150 W Broadway, Vancouver, V6K 4L9, Canada. Tel: (604) 536-3880

The Southern Cross Academy of Astrology, PO Box 781147, Sandton, SA 2146 (South Africa) Tel: 11-468-1157; Fax: 11-468-1522

Periodicals

American Astrology Magazine, PO Box 140713, Staten Island, NY 10314-0713. e-mail: am.astrology@genie.gies,com

The Journal of the Seasons, PO Box 5266, Wellesley St, Auckland 1, New Zealand. Tel/fax: (0)9-410-8416

The Federation of Australian Astrologers Bulletin, PO Box 159, Stepney, SA 5069. Tel/fax: 8-331-3057

Aspects, PO Box 2968, Rivonia 2128, SA (South Africa)
Tel: 11-864-1436

Realta, The Journal of the Irish Astrological Association, 4 Quay Street, Galway, Ireland. Available from IAA, 193, Lwr Rathmines Rd, Dublin 6, Ireland.

Astrological Association, 396 Caledonian Road, London, N1 1DN. Tel: (UK code) 0171 700 3746; Fax: 0171 700 6479. Bi-monthly journal issued.